Plays by
Janet Neipris

Broadway Play Publishing Inc

New York

BroadwayPlayPub.com

Cover photo: Don Wille

First printing: March 2000
I S B N: 978-0-88145-166-5

Book design: Marie Donovan
Copy editing: Michele Travis
Typeface: Palatino

CONTENTS

ABOUT THE AUTHOR

Janet Neipris was born in Boston, graduated from Tufts University
and received an M A in English from Simmons College and an M F A in
Playwriting from Brandeis University. Her plays have been produced at
theaters in the U S and internationally, including the Manhattan Theater
Club, Arena Stage, in DC, Studio Theater in DC, Goodman Theater in
Chicago, Center Stage in Baltimore, Milwaukee Repertory, Pittsburgh
Public Theater, Manhattan Punch Line Theater, The Women's Project in
New York, and the Annenberg Center in Philadelphia. In spring, 1995,
her play A SMALL DELEGATION was produced by the China Youth
Arts Theater in Beijing, directed by Shi Zheng Chen.

Her other plays include STATUES, EXHIBITION, THE BRIDGE AT BEL
HARBOUR, OUT OF ORDER, SEPARATIONS, NOTES ON A LIFE
(music and lyrics), SOUTHERNMOST TIP, 703 WALK HILL, NATIVES,
and a collection of one-act plays, ACTS OF LOVE.

A composer as well as a playwright, she co-authored and wrote the score
for the musical JEREMY AND THE THINKING MACHINE. She also has
written music for Kevin O'Morrison's play, REQUIEM, music for Circle
Rep, New York, and scored music for piano and flute for the Sharon,
CT Playhouse production of Arthur Miller's DEATH OF A SALESMAN,
called by *The New York Times* "translucent", "haunting and delicate,
capturing the pains and charms of Miller's work". Born into a family
of musicians going back three generations, the playwright's father was
both a part-time cantor and a salesman.

Janet Neipris has also written for film, television, National Public Radio,
and the B B C.

As a Professor at New York University, she has served as chair of the
Department of Dramatic Writing from 1983-1999. She has been active in
international education, teaching writers in China, Indonesia, Australia,
England, and Italy. A recipient of grants, including a Schubert Fellowship,
an NEA in Playwriting in 1981 and 1997, a Rockefeller Grant to Bellagio,
a W Alton Jones Production Grant, a U S I A grant, and Virginia Center
for The Creative Arts grants, she is a member of PEN, the Writers Guild
of America East, and the Dramatists Guild Council.

PREFACE

The beginnings of plays, the source of that river from which they flow, has always fascinated me as a writer. The origins of every play are as various as they are similar, as elusive as they seem clear, and as magical as they appear grounded. The three plays in this volume differ vastly in their topographies and genesis; what unites them, however, is the place where they land—call it home.

THE AGREEMENT, a comedy about separation, was originally commissioned by PBS Radio. Every play posits a question. As in Robert Frost's poem, *The Oven Bird*, the question THE AGREEMENT asks is what to make of a diminished thing. When you separate from a long relationship, you are leaving behind more than an address. What about the ties to a galaxy of family and friends, a chunk of your biography? Do you lose that too? One of the characters in THE AGREEMENT says "I liked his family; it was him I didn't like." Funny? Yes. Serious? A direct shot from the heart. The argument over possessions in the dissolution of a marriage is never about carpets or teacups, but more about the unravelling of any work of art or love.

It was a deliberate choice in THE AGREEMENT to deal with disconnection through comedy, so when, towards the end, the goods are being divided frantically, including the children, the play concludes with a quiet anguish.

In an early staging of two one-act plays, STATUES and THE BRIDGE AT BEL HARBOUR at the Goodman Theatre in Chicago, Greg Mosher directed Judith Ivey in a chillingly funny production. It managed to dance delicately on the edge of light and dark. This *chiaroscuro*, that technique of Renaissance painters describing the abrupt changes from light to shadow which occur when a figure stands in bright light, would eventually color all my work. Was that purposeful? As a playwright I never chose a style, but, instead, it chose me. If there is such a thing as original voice, it lies in the unconscious, fed by our passions and instincts.

ALMOST IN VEGAS started its life as THE DESERT, also written originally for P B S. The play is set in Las Vegas, the neon heart of America. Somewhere I read that flowers in the desert only bloom once a year, and it stuck with me. So, in trying to locate this play about American icons, about the myths that both bind and blind us to our longing, the idea for ALMOST IN VEGAS began to grow. The frame would be the anticipated performance of Frank Sinatra at a Las Vegas hotel. The play would take place over a weekend, when crowds would gather in anticipation of hearing "the voice", but something would delay his performance. Only on the third draft of the play did I realize the mythologized hero would never show up. Not long after, Sinatra was dead.

The incident that sparked ALMOST IN VEGAS was a woman friend, a serious artist, who called at the last minute cancelling a plan we had one Saturday night because "something better came up". What did that mean, "better"? When and why did we become callous and rapacious? How did longing affect loyalty? In an age when women pledged their newly found Friedan-Steinem sisterhood, how truly rooted was this alliancer? If the play was about women's friendship on one level, it was more about the desperation of fracture and isolation.

ALMOST IN VEGAS also was conceived as a comedy, but one with a dark underbelly. The scene where Alma is dancing with Louis, brilliantly played by April Shawhan and David Little in the original production at Pittsburgh Public Theatre, is always painful to watch, so still in its emptiness. That it concludes well in the desert for these characters is due to the basic comedic tone. We are funny and moving, powerful and finally sad in our desire for connection.

A SMALL DELEGATION was based on an incident in Beijing two summers before Tiananmen Square. As a group of four American screenwriters, including Richard Walter, head of U C L A Screenwriting, I was invited to China to teach the next generation of Chinese screenwriters. It also was an attempt, following the Cultural Revolution, to better relations between the U S and China. It was Richard who aptly named our foursome "the small delegation". Our students, incidentally, would go on to become the talented "fifth generation" of Chinese screenwriters, including Chen Kaige and Zhang Yimou.

The play grew out of a politically incorrect gift I gave my translator. Because so many books had been destroyed or "misplaced" during the Cultural Revolution, I decided to give my new friend in Beijing, a western educated woman, a valuable book. We had been advised by the State Department to bring gifts, as the Chinese, by custom, would greet us with many presents. Protocol, which was never directly stated, was that all members of the institute where we were teaching should receive gifts of equal value. The translator subsequently got into trouble for accepting the "special" book. If she hadn't accepted it, however, she would have insulted "the visiting Americans". Catch-22 in Beijing.

At first glance, post-Cultural Revolution China seemed free, but the longer we stayed, I had the feeling things were not as free as they appeared. The differences between East and West were more complex than could be found from reading history books. Meanwhile, the idea for a play was growing.

A SMALL DELEGATION is the story of a group of Americans who come to teach in China the summer of 1988. It's the story of two women, the American professor, Remy, and her translator, Sun, and the eventual impossibility of their friendship. Remy, in meaning to do good, but failing to understand the cultural differences between East and West, ends up ruining the life of her Chinese friend. If the play is about good intentions gone wrong, it's also about the impossibility of any two cultures or people wholly understanding each other.

Of all the areas on the stage, the hardest to locate and the most important to reveal is the dangerous space where two lives touch.

A SMALL DELEGATION, after productions in the U.S., went to Beijing where it was directed by my friend and colleague, Chen Shi-Zheng. It was closed down after the first presentation due to "cultural differences" but not before we met with a group of prominent Chinese critics after the performance, as is customary in China. The translator for this epic meeting was none other than my original translator, the one who had sparked the idea of the play eight years before. So, there in Beijing, I had come full circle and home.

Each play in this volume was launched from a different place, yet each came to touch down on the same landing space. In the end, the first draft of A SMALL DELEGATION, completed just before the Tiananmen Square massacre in June 1989, turned out to be what all my plays are about—the fragility of human connection.

As for the plays in this volume, each is as a child. You, as the author, give them the best you have, and then wish them well on their journey in the world.

Janet Neipris
March 2000
New York City

DEDICATION

For my daughters Cynthia, Carolyn, and Ellen,
and my husband Donald

A SMALL
DELEGATION

A SMALL DELEGATION was written with a Rockefeller Fellowship to Bellagio, an N E A grant, and first produced under a W Alton Jones grant. The play opened at the Harold Prince Theater, Annenberg Center, Philadelphia, in June 1992, and was produced by The Philadelphia Festival Theater for New Plays. The cast and creative contributors were:

REMY .... Joyce Lynn O'Conner
SUN .... Freda Foh Shen
PHILIP .... Terry Layman
ELIZABETH .... Anne Newhall
MEI YEN .... Tina Chen
COMRADE WU .... Mel Duane Gionson
SHERWOOD/PASSPORT OFFICER .... Shi-Zheng Chen
LILI .... Bai Ling

Director ....Susan H Schulman
Design .... Ming Cho Lee
Assistant designer .... Karen Teneyck
Costumes .... Vickie Esposito
Lighting .... Curt Senie
Original music composition .... Tan Dun
Musical direction & choreography .... Shi-Zheng Chen

A revised script of A SMALL DELEGATION was produced in Beijing in April 1995, produced by the China Youth Arts Theater under the direction of Shi-Zheng Chen. The cast were:

REMY .... Wang Li Yun
(SUN) LIU XIN .... Yang Qing
PHILIP .... Shi Wei Jian
ELIZABETH .... Zhang Xiao Li
MEI YEN .... Zhang Ying
OLD WU .... Chen Qiang
SHERWOOD/PASSPORT OFFICER .... Wang Nan
LILI ....Wang Qing Mei

The Beijing production was made possible with the help of the following: The Asia Society, Asian Cultural Council, The China Institute, Geraldine and John Kunstadter Foundation, New York University and Starr Foundation.

CHARACTERS

REMY, *an American professor, a woman in her early thirties*
SUN, *a Chinese translator, a woman in her early thirties*
PHILIP, *an American professor, about forty*
ELIZABETH, PHILIP'*s wife, a doctor*
MEI YEN, *Chinese government official, in charge of Summer Institute*
COMRADE WU, *Chinese government tour guide; he is in his mid-forties*
SHERWOOD, *Chinese graduate student and engineer*
LILI, *a young Chinese actress*
PASSPORT OFFICER, *a young man*
MUSICIANS

Casting note: PASSPORT OFFICER *may be played by same actor as* SHERWOOD.
The MUSICIANS *may be played by* LILI *and* SHERWOOD *or* PASSPORT OFFICER.

SCENES

ACT ONE

On The Great Wall—Summer 1988
Scene One—*Temple of the Sleeping Buddha, near Beijing, courtyard, early morning, June l988*
Scene Two—*Classroom, immediately following*
Scene Three—*Hotel room, Beijing, early that same evening*
Scene Four—*Great Wall Sheraton Hotel, Beijing, banquet hall, later that evening*
Scene Five—*MEI YEN's office, a week later*
Scene Six—*The Friendship Store, Beijing, a few weeks later*
Scene Seven—*Beihai Park, Beijing, mid-June*
Scene Eight—*Tiananmen Square, Beijing, later that week*
Scene Nine—*Temple of the Sleeping Buddha, the next morning*
Scene Ten—*Classroom, immediately following*
Scene Eleven—*Hotel room, Beijing, three days later*
Scene Twelve—*Hotel lobby, Beijing, immediately following*
Scene Thirteen—*A street in Beijing, the same night*
On The Great Wall

ACT TWO

Scene One—*Courtyard, Beihai Park, sunrise, the next morning*
Scene Two—*Forbidden City, later the same day, noon*
On The Great Wall
Scene Three—*P R C passport office, Beijing, the next day, early morning*
Scene Four—*Temple of the Sleeping Buddha, classroom, the same morning, the fourth of July*
Scene Five—*Tiananmen Square, the next afternoon*
Scene Six—*A tearoom, Beijing, several days later*
Scene Seven—*Hotel room, Shanghai, three days later*
Scene Eight—*Classroom, Beijing, three days later*
Scene Nine—*Ming tombs, Xian, one week later, late July*
Scene Ten—*P R C passport office, Beijing, two hours later, the same day*
Scene Eleven—*Public Security Bureau, detention room, Beijing, several hours later*
Scene Twelve—*Hotel room, Beijing, a few days later, late at night, the first of August*
On The Great Wall

"They knew themselves as residents of the Celestial Empire; their ruler they called the Son of Heaven. Surrounded by peoples less culturally advanced, they felt they were a kind of chosen people, chosen not by God but by virtue of their superior attainments. Foreigners were known as barbarians. And the land of China was called Zhongguo, or Central Kingdom. It was a luminous domain, the global seat of civilization and of ethical conduct; it was quite simply—the center of the earth."
Richard Bernstein, *From The Center Of The Earth, The Search For the Truth About China*

ACT ONE

(The action of the play takes place on The Great Wall of China in the summer of 1988, and in Beijing, Xi'an, and Shanghai during that same summer. The central image of the play is a large simple circle, representing a circular section of The Great Wall.)

(The continuous action of the play is the climb on the wall, intercut with a series of scenes during that summer, played out on points on the inside of the circle.)

(Little scenery is needed. Just a suggestion of reality. Only the scenes on The Great Wall are out of sequence in time, and meant to be as in a dream. Scenes on The Great Wall should be lit differently, as if the clock had been stopped.)

(Lights fade up. In the background is heard, as if in a distance, a flute. REMY, an American professor, about thirty, and SUN, a Chinese translator, thirty, are at D S center, six o'clock on the circle. REMY wears large sunglasses and SUN wears a traditional cone shaped bamboo hat.)

On The Great Wall

(REMY and SUN D S center on the Great Wall.)

REMY: *(Wiping herself with a handkerchief)* It must be a hundred degrees out today.

SUN: Only ninety-eight.

REMY: I should have brought a hat. American women, you know, have been warned to stay out of the sun because of cancer.

SUN: You mean the Government doesn't allow it?

REMY: *(Out of breath, stopping, and SUN stops along with her)* No. You can do whatever you want. It just may be bad for you.

SUN: In China, we're governed more by rules. For example, you are not a hero until you've climbed the Great Wall.

REMY: In the U S we go to the top of the Empire State Building or ride down the Colorado River on a raft.

SUN: Is it true that in New York you can order pizza on the telephone and it's brought to your house?

REMY: Chinese too. You call, and ten minutes later, Boom! Pork dumplings and lo mein. They deliver on bicycles, and promptly.

SUN: Oh sure. We're an obedient culture. Congenial too. For instance, notice my quick smile. Sun, like the sun. *(Taking off her hat, offering it to REMY)* Here, take my hat. Let's begin the climb.

(REMY takes the bamboo hat and the two start to walk, silently at first, SUN leading the way. Note that they should begin D S center, six o'clock on the circle, so that by the end of the play, they have completed a full circle.)

REMY: How many steps until we get to the top?

SUN: Fourteen hundred. But when we're there, it's extraordinary— many springs, large evergreen trees, wildflowers.

REMY: This trip is the farthest I've ever been from home.

SUN: On this wall is the *only* place *high* enough, and *far* enough away, so one feels at home...so I can breathe without asking permission.

(Beat)

REMY: Is it a mistake to think we could be friends this summer?

SUN: No. But I think for good face, we should stick to the group. It's protocol and also politic.

(Lights down on them)

(End of scene)

Scene One

(Time: June 1988, early morning)

(Place: The courtyard of the temple of the Sleeping Buddha, in the hills, outside of Beijing. The open flagstone courtyard, with a single banyan tree, is surrounded by several small buildings used for conferences, and a temple which houses a figure of a sleeping Buddha. SUN, dressed in a simple skirt and flowered blouse, stands in the courtyard waiting. The sound of a car driving up.)

SUN: They're here! There they are!

(MEI YEN, a woman in her late forties, with long dark hair, pulled back in a pony tail, and dressed in a cotton summer suit, comes walking quickly into the courtyard, looking towards the front gate)

MEI YEN: *(To SUN)* Ask them if they want to pee, then offer them some orange soda. *(Beat)* I like the tall *(Please adapt for specific production)* one's earrings.

(REMY, in high heels, sheer stockings, a silk dress, and dangling earrings enters with a book bag, followed by COMRADE WU, dressed efficiently but impeccably,

together with a much wilted PHILIP *and* ELIZABETH MILTON. MEI YEN *comes forward.)*

REMY: You must be Mei Yen. *(Shaking* MEI YEN's *hand)* I'm Professor Remy Martin, American Literature. *(Turning to others)* This is Professor Milton... his wife, Elizabeth. Philip's in the History Department at N Y U.

PHILIP: European.

ELIZABETH: Medieval, actually, between the Greeks and the Italian Renaissance.

MEI YEN: *(Exchanging handshakes)* Welcome to the Summer Institute. Welcome to the Temple of the Sleeping Buddha. How was your flight?

REMY: They stopped us in Shanghai at bloody three in the morning; and when we were coming through customs in Beijing, they went through our books.

PHILIP: They confiscated one of my magazines.

COMRADE WU: There was a question it was perhaps pornographic.

ELIZABETH: It was *The New York Review of Books.*

COMRADE WU: We'll get it back later.

PHILIP: How?

MEI YEN: Later. *(Then introducing* SUN*)* This will be your translator while you're here.

SUN: *(Coming forward, extending her hand)* Sun, like the sun.

REMY: *(Shaking it)* Remy, like the cognac. My parents were in Paris when I was conceived, and thought it was adorable to name me for an after dinner drink.

PHILIP: I speak Chinese, so I won't be needing a translator.

ELIZABETH: Philip is fluent in six languages, not counting English.

MEI YEN: Very good.

REMY: What a ride here from the Jing Jang Hotel! And I thought New York taxicabs were scary.

MEI YEN: There's a lot to contend with on the streets of Beijing. It's the question of the equestrian versus the pedestrian.

REMY: Yes. Mr Wu, in fact ...

MEI YEN: *(Correcting her)* Comrade Wu.

REMY: Comrade Wu, yes, told the driver to slow down. We came to some sheep in the road, and he just kept plowing through, giving them the horn, and the people and animals, carts with cabbages, grandma on a bicycle, carrying a chicken on one handlebar and a grandchild on the other, just got out of the way, parted like the Red Sea to let us through.

MEI YEN: They could see you were foreign visitors.

SUN: The people manage to escape, but sometimes there's an accident.

COMRADE WU: Like when Nixon was here.

SUN: *(Squealing)* Oh yes, the pigs! What a sight! Right on Janhuachi Road. Pigs everywhere!

REMY: I thought I'd lose my insides.

ELIZABETH: I kept my eyes closed all the way.

PHILIP: I kept my legs crossed. I've had to urinate ever since we left the hotel.

SUN: Then you should use the toilet first. The students are in the classrooms waiting.

MEI YEN: Remy will be teaching in the Flower Pagoda. Philip will be in the Great Hall. *(Beat)* Very good. And Professor Milton has been appointed Head of your delegation. He sits to the left of the Guest of Honor at banquets and makes the first toast.

SUN: By tradition the Leader is always a male scholar.

PHILIP: I told Mei Yen, I'm honored.

REMY: *(To PHILIP)* You didn't tell *me*.

MEI YEN: We asked Philip to be secret; things can change.

COMRADE WU: Kuai. Bing-bang.

REMY: God, yes, bing-bang.

ELIZABETH: Phillip's been reviewing his lectures all the way over, from Dante to Disraeli.

MEI YEN: "The East is a career," Mr Disraeli said. Before the Cultural Revolution, of course, that was read.

SUN: Which is why we're excited about your visit. Some of our books were misplaced during the C R.

COMRADE WU: Temporarily taken by the Red Guard.

MEI YEN: In the Cultural Revolution. But then they were certainly returned.

COMRADE WU: Most were returned.

SUN: But some were lost. So this generation knows little, for example, by William Wordsworth or Walt Whitman.

REMY: *(Excited)* Walt Whitman! That's my first lesson! *(Taking a leather volume out)* Look at this! Walt Whitman. That's a coincidence. I think that's fate. Isn't that fate?

MEI YEN: A question for the gods; but Whitman, of course, is admired here, now in 1988, for his views on democracy.

REMY: *(Taking a breath, becoming more formal, but exhilarated)* We hope our small delegation can share with our Chinese colleagues, our American spirit, the pioneering spirit. That's what we bring across the ocean, from west to east, building a bridge of new friendship....

PHILIP: Ditto.

MEI YEN: Our expectations are simpler. We want you to teach us whatever we can learn. *(Pointing to REMY's book)* And that's a handsome book. Is it an original edition?

REMY: It was my father's. He was an eminent Whitman scholar.

SUN: *(Breaking in)* We should go. It's important to start on time.

REMY: How long should the lecture be?

MEI YEN: Not over four hours.

PHILIP: Not over four hours.

COMRADE WU: In the afternoon we've planned a trip to the cloisonné factory.

MEI YEN: We've made special arrangements. Last year, Professor Nick Hunter, from U C L A bought two large vases there—so big, he had to buy an extra suitcase to cart them home.

COMRADE WU: And we have permission to see Chairman Mao.

SUN: He's in a see-through box.

REMY: If it's okay, I'd rather see The Forbidden City.

COMRADE WU: The Forbidden City is *next* week. This afternoon we visit the cloisonné factory. Any questions about coming or going, ask me. Tonight we'll go to the Great Wall Sheraton where there'll be a Texas-style barbecue in your honor.

MEI YEN: The cloisonné factory is famous; all the work is done by hand. *(To REMY)* And, by the way, those are earrings to be admired.

REMY: They're street jewelry. They sell them in the streets in New York.

MEI YEN: We sell food on our streets.

REMY: So do we.

PHILIP: Hot dogs.

COMRADE WU: And this isn't always true that we eat dogs. It's a quite vicious rumor.

ELIZABETH: *(To COMRADE WU)* I'm sure. In the morning I like to run. Is there a park where I can run?

COMRADE WU: No. I don't think so. But there's sunrise discoing in a nearby park where you can go for aerobic exercise. They do the tango there. It's the newest rage. *(Pointing to the right)* And the washrooms are *that* way.

MEI YEN: On Sunday we'll climb the Great Wall.

SUN: Unless it rains.

MEI YEN: Then we'll take umbrellas.

(End of scene)

Scene Two

(Time: Immediately following)

(Place: Classroom, Temple of the Sleeping Buddha. REMY and SUN sit side by side at a desk. On the desk is a Thermos of water. REMY gets up, moves D S, faces audience, as though we were the class. As she speaks, SUN translates into Chinese, waiting for REMY to pause. The speeches can overlap.)

REMY: *The American Spirit,* as found in the poetry of Walt Whitman, born May 31, 1819, died March 26th, 1892.

(Pause)

SUN: *Wa er te Huìte màn chu sheng yu yi ba yi; iu nian wu yuè san shí yi haò qùishi yú yi ba; iu èr nian sán yuè èr shí liù ri.*

REMY: When I first read Walt Whitman, it was summer and I was in Italy.

SUN: *(Holding up her hand, signaling REMY to stop so she can translate) (Chinese translation)*

REMY: And because I was twenty-two— *(Holding up two fingers twice)* —and in a foreign country, afraid to be alone, it was the only connection with my own country—the language.

SUN: *Yin wè wo zai waìguo, hài pà gu dú, yu yán shi wo he Wo de Zuquó baochí lianxi de weí yí tújìng.*

(Imitating REMY, holding up two fingers)

SUN: *(Pause, scanning the class, sighting a raised hand)* A student would like to know, what was Whitman's approach to the Civil War?

REMY: He saw Lincoln as the savior of the slaves, which he was.

SUN: *(Chinese translation. Pause, scanning class)* Someone has asked if it was true that your President, Thomas Jefferson, kept slaves, although he professed to be against slavery.

REMY: *(Obviously rattled)* Yes. It's true. Well it's complex.

SUN: *(To the class) Shi de, zhe shi zhen de, dan shi, zhe li hen fu za. (Then to* REMY*)* Here in China, we're accustomed to doing what we say. This way, the action matches the word.

REMY: *(To* SUN*)* You're never hypocritical then.

SUN: Only in our hearts. We've perfected the art of biaotai—giving a performance.

REMY: Tell them Jefferson had slaves, but in his heart, he was against it. Then say... *(Quoting Whitman, and as she does,* SUN *translates simultaneously, as she knows the poem)* "I celebrate myself, and sing myself
And what I assume you shall assume"

SUN: *"Wo zanmei wo ziji, gechang wo ziji/Wo chengdan ni ye jiang chengdan"*

REMY: The individual means everything to Whitman...*privacy....*

SUN: *(To* REMY*)* I can't translate that.

REMY: Why not?

SUN: There's no word for privacy in Chinese. Just go on quickly. Cover up.

REMY: *(To class)* So, Whitman, spent most of his time alone in a room.

SUN: It's better not to say that either. No one has a room of their own in Beijing, except for punishment.

(Lights down)

(Lights up. A few hours later, a weary REMY*,* SUN *fans herself.)*

REMY: ...And so, as Confucius said, "I transmit, but I do not originate."

SUN: Zheng ru kong zi shuo de: *"Shu er bu zuo."* *(Beat)* They liked that, that you quoted from us, sixth century B C.

REMY: The thing about China is it's so damn authentically ancient. *(Turning to* SUN*)* Am I done yet?

SUN: Good. Four hours, ten minutes. Overachiever.

REMY: *(Much relieved, to class)* At our next class we'll discuss the works of Henry Wadsworth Longfellow.

SUN: *(Chinese translation)* —Longfellow *(Applause)* They're pleased. They admire Longfellow because he rhymes. Now stand up. The lecture is over. The students won't leave until you do. Respect for authority.

REMY: For the teacher.

SUN: The *American* teacher.

(They stand, turning D S, as COMRADE WU *and* ELIZABETH *enter with teacups, chatting, at far end of courtyard.)*

REMY: *(Softly, to* SUN*)* Elizabeth came to assist Philip with his slides.

SUN: I thought you had Women's Liberation in your country.

REMY: We do. Elizabeth's a public health doctor. She works in an AIDS clinic. But this is her vacation, so it's a relief just to be a wife.

SUN: She looks unsure.

REMY: She's made of steel. She lives with Philip.

SUN: The fine art of performance again.

REMY: Women are experts; *which means* I have no idea what *I'm* saying to the class is what *you're* saying to the class.

SUN: Unless we plan to trust each other. *(Beat)* I sometimes think about going to a brave city like New York. There are more books at Columbia University, I hear, than in the entire world.

REMY: If you come, our apartment has a pull-out couch. And you can see Central Park out the window.

SUN: Don't tempt me...But, like everyone, I enjoy a good daydream.

(REMY begins packing up her books and lecture notes. SUN, watching each book disappear into REMY's bag)

SUN: We owned a copy of *Leaves Of Grass* which was my mother's, but it was misplaced in the Cultural Revolution. But that's the past.

REMY: *(Pause, then frantically searching in the depths of her enormous bag for the Whitman book, finding it, holding it out)* Why don't you take the book. Here. Take it. Take the Whitman. It would make me happy.

SUN: I think absolutely not. This is a very valuable book.

REMY: *(Insisting)* No. It's a gift. I know where to get another one. *(Pushing it on her)* Look, at home I wanted all this stuff. Now my house is full of stuff. You have to take it.

(SUN stands frozen. Then REMY quickly pushes the book into SUN's hand as MEI YEN and PHILIP join ELIZABETH, and COMRADE WU in the Courtyard)

SUN: *(To REMY)* Books are still scarce, since the Gang of Four. We think they ate them for dinner, since they all had big bellies. We intellectuals are hungry for books. Others dream of Sony T Vs. *(Pause)* Those are nice too.

(SUN quickly stuffs the book into her bag. They both stand, Moving D S, towards Courtyard)

SUN: *(Whispering, as they walk)* See Mei Yen? She's a single woman. She lives permanently without her husband and independent. *(Beat)* Are you married?"

REMY: To a historian. He teaches with Philip. *(Beat)* We're on a trial separation. I'm here, he's there.

MEI YEN: *(Walking up to them)* So how did it go? Philip was a great success, especially with the ladies.

REMY: The students wrote down every word. I mean, not everything's a pearl.

(SUN *is silent. Perhaps* MEI YEN *has seen the book*)

ELIZABETH: Comrade Wu took me to see the discoing in the Park. There were dozens of people doing the tango.

COMRADE WU: The old ones still do T'ai Chi.

SUN: Out of habit.

MEI YEN: Out of tradition.

COMRADE WU: I taught Elizabeth "White Crane Spreads Wings."

(ELIZABETH *assumes the above position,* COMRADE WU *joins her*)

MEI YEN: One of our most direct moves, because it takes concentration, is "Step Forward And Punch." It's a warning position—Don't cross this line, or you may find my fist in your mouth. (*Assuming the position*) It's why we built a wall. Like your Robert Frost says, "Good fences make good neighbors."

(*End of scene*)

Scene Three

(*Time: Early that evening*)

(*Place:* REMY's *hotel room, Beijing. An open suitcase is on a bed.* REMY, *in a bathrobe, a towel around her just washed hair, goes through her suitcase, frantically looking for something.* PHILIP, *already dressed for the evening, smokes a cigarette and paces.* ELIZABETH *is writing in her journal.*)

REMY: How was I to know we're expected to bring everyone a present? No one told me.

PHILIP: They told *me.*

REMY: The History Department is just more efficient.

PHILIP: Or maybe I'm a better listener.

REMY: How would you like my fist in your mouth?

PHILIP: We brought these Statue of Liberty thingamajigs. (*Getting out of his bag a bunch of souvenir Statue of Liberty statuettes.*)

ELIZABETH: Are those tacky *or what?*

REMY: (*Now really rattled, plowing through her suitcase*) Maybe I can give Comrade Wu my watch. (*Holding up her watch*)

ELIZABETH: (*Continuing to write in her journal*) Too extravagant.

REMY: My belt then! *(Pulling out a belt)* Genuine American. I got it in Montana. It has a buffalo on it.

PHILIP: I heard these welcoming banquets are very formal.

REMY: *(Still looking through suitcase, pulling out...)* A scarf. Jesus, Ted bought this for me in Venice. *(Holding up the scarf)* What the hell! For Mei Yen. *(Wrapping scarf in tissue)* What about Bic ball point pens for the drivers?

ELIZABETH: Too cheap.

REMY: *(Grabbing her wallet)* Perfect then! Plain old dollar bills. The drivers will love it. *(Waving bills)* And think of the symbolism. *(Beat)* I gave Sun my Whitman book.

PHILIP: Why did you do *that*? It's a first edition.

REMY: Look at all this stuff we came with. *(Pulling clothes out)* Sweaters, skirts, jackets, silk underwear! Did you see how simply they dress? I'm not wearing any of my jewelry. I feel like a conspicuous consumptive.

PHILIP: Let me assure you, you're just a run of the mill capitalist like the rest of us.

REMY: What are you going to say for your toast tonight at our Great Wall Bar-B-Q?

PHILIP: You're pissed. It was either you or I to head our Delegation.

ELIZABETH: Even though Remy's senior faculty.

PHILIP: You heard their tradition—the male scholar.

ELIZABETH: Please don't be an academic prick. Or do the two go together?

PHILIP: *(To ELIZABETH)* I hope they serve bear's paws tonight, and you can't refuse, because if you do, it's an insult, and they never give you anything again.

ELIZABETH: We should leave for the barbecue. You know they're there waiting for us early so they won't be late.

REMY: And I may give Sun some of my jewelry.

ELIZABETH: That's like saying "Here we are, us rich Americans." I need to get dressed. I plan to talk Comrade Wu into letting me visit a hospital. What interests me is how they're treating infectious disease. I'll bet more aggressively than we are. How do you say "please" in Chinese?

PHILIP: Ching.

ELIZABETH: *(Exits, repeating)* "Ching."

PHILIP: Did you know Elizabeth has refused to sleep with me? She says I've become "uncreative"

REMY: You should try a sex therapist or a book. *(Beat)* What are you going to say for your toast?

PHILIP: I don't know.

REMY: Then say "gan bei" *(Lifting her glass)* Bottoms up!

(End of scene)

Scene Four

(Time: Later that evening)

(Place: The Great Wall Sheraton Hotel. There is a Texas style barbecue banquet as a welcome for the Americans. Gathered, drinks in hand, are MEI YEN, COMRADE WU, SUN, REMY, PHILIP, *and* ELIZABETH. *Two musicians, a man and a woman, (LILI) play traditional Chinese instruments. Strains of "Oh Susannah" are heard.* MEI YEN *wears the scarf* REMY *has given her.)*

MEI YEN: *(Holding her glass)* Dear delegation, hello. *Ni hao.* Welcome to the Great Wall Sheraton. We've prepared a Texas style barbecue to say how happy we are you're here. And entertainment by the quite famous Zhou Minh and Miss Lili Chan. *(Clinking her glass against* PHILIP's*)* Cheers. *(All drink, then referring to the liquor)* First, I should caution you about our maotai. It's known to be lethal for foreigners.

PHILIP: *(Holding up his glass)* Gan bei.

(He clinks glasses with MEI YEN, *then all clink with each other, and so on)*

MEI YEN: *(Clinking again, drinking)* Gan bei! Before we attack our Kentucky Fried Chicken—our newest store in the P R C *(People's Republic of China),* we should tell the saying, "Eat the fish before the fish eats you." The Chinese have a saying for everything.

COMRADE WU: Later, we're planning a more traditional banquet.

SUN: Two thousand year old eggs and drunken chicken.

REMY: *(Holding up her glass, trying to think of something very Chinese)* "To spring, to the bloom of a hundred flowers."

(Clinking glasses with all. There is silence, then slowly the Chinese drink. REMY *has obviously said something wrong)*

COMRADE WU: *(Raising his glass to the Americans in a toast. There's a great relief as the silence is broken. This next section should all go fairly rapidly.)* "Remember the Red River Valley"!

(They all clink and drink)

ELIZABETH: *(Raising her glass)* "Remember the Alamo!"

(All clink and drink. COMRADE WU *refills glasses)*

SUN: *(Raising her glass)* Sunshine on my shoulders makes me happy... John Denver, "Rocky Mountain High."

(Clink and drink)

PHILIP: *(Raising glass)* To the wisdom of the east...

MEI YEN: *(Raising glass)* To the riches of the west... *(Putting glass down)* Let's eat. Dig in. *(Handing* PHILIP *a newspaper)* Oh, and Philip, *The New York Review of Books* was declared non-controversial.

(COMRADE WU and PHILIP EXIT followed by MEI YEN and ELIZABETH. They move U S on the circle to a table set with fried chicken. Lights fade as they serve themselves, and up on SUN and REMY who remain behind.)

REMY: What did I say wrong?

SUN: Nothing. *(Then, without missing a beat)* I think Mei Yen saw you give me the book. Did you give *her* a book?

REMY: A scarf. The one she's wearing. It's a very good scarf.

SUN: Not good enough. It's not a book.

REMY: Then I'll give her a book.

SUN: But it won't be the *same* book. It's tricky. China is a plate of sand. *(Beat)* Remy's wrong-saying... "Let a hundred flowers grow." The government said the same thing once, "Let flowers grow, Speak any words you want." So we put up posters on a Democracy wall. *Then* the government said "We don't like these ideas," and the soldiers came and tore them down, and you couldn't do the ideas anymore. It reminds us not to be foolish. *(Beat)* But, *xie xie.*

REMY: What does that mean?

SUN: Thank you for my Whitman.

REMY: *Xie xie.*

SUN: *Bu xie.* You're welcome. And I think it's stupid how they made a barbecue. I could be punished for saying that. It was Mei Yen's idea. She enjoys being an original thinker.

REMY: Is this an original thought, Sun? You'd like to leave someday?

SUN: I want to *stay*; I want to *leave*. My unruly ancestors are sometimes demons. But we're missing the Kentucky chicken.

REMY: What if we choose instead to go to the restaurant here in the hotel?

SUN: *Choose.* This is a new foreign concept. And have American drinks? Bloody Mary?

REMY: You bet! I invite you! You're my guest.

SUN: You bet! And after we could ride up and down in the glass elevators. *(Pause)* Then everyone would see us alone. *(A hesitation, then)* I invite you instead to my house for dinner. Sunday. *(Writing on a piece of paper, handing it to* REMY *secretly)* My address. Later I'll draw you a map. *(Excitedly)* You'll meet my husband and son and I'll cook *haizhe pi,* jellyfish. Close your eyes and it tastes like scallops. And you won't be surprised by my son. He's one of the new rascals. He watches television and dreams of riding a motorcycle.

REMY: *Xie xie, xie xie, xie xie.*

SUN: We better teach you a new word.

(End of scene)

Scene Five

(Time: A week later)

(Place: MEI YEN's *office.* MEI YEN *is seated behind a desk.* SUN *sits in a chair.)*

MEI YEN: What did you say when you were given the book?

SUN: I said "Thank you." I said "This is a very valuable book."

MEI YEN: Of course. You had to be polite.

SUN: Of course I had to be polite.

MEI YEN: But you didn't report the book. It wasn't listed in the register.

SUN: Because I had mistaken information.

MEI YEN: That can happen.

SUN: It happened to me that Professor Remy said the book *was* valuable. But I was told it *wasn't.* So she was misinformed. Otherwise, I would have reported such a valuable gift.

MEI YEN: Of course. *(She takes the Whitman book from her lap and opens it on the table)* Only this book of Walt Whitman *is* valuable. It's a first edition. *(Beat)* Who told you the book wasn't valuable?

SUN: A bookseller near Fu Xinmen Street. I don't remember exactly where. I neglected to get his name. But it's very clear to me he was a stupid man and didn't give me the right details. But now I know. I was right in the first place and should have reported this important gift, a first edition of *Leaves of Grass* by Walt Whitman.

MEI YEN: Don't get too involved. It's only a summer romance. Be honey-tongued but correct. You wouldn't want to be branded a spy mistakenly.

SUN: Appearances.

MEI YEN: Just caution. You're up for a promotion at the university. Comrade Wu is a true party guy. You have a short memory.

SUN: For God's sakes, it's 1988! Things have turned around! Our doors are open.

MEI YEN: Don't be stupid. Don't be an ostrich.

SUN: I already died once. What could I fear?

(Beat)

MEI YEN: I heard you were reconciled with your father.

SUN: It's true.

MEI YEN: He must have been angry or sad.

SUN: He understood. I simply was misinformed by the Red Guards, like most of us. They said "Your father is bad," and I believed them. *(Beat)* In America, you know, since Gloria Steinem, women have loyal and giggling friendships.

MEI YEN: That's not a luxury we can afford.

SUN: Why not?

(Beat)

MEI YEN: *(Considers it)* We have higher pursuits.

SUN: Like what?

MEI YEN: Sun, one could be exasperated by you! *(Beat)* Here are four books to translate. *(Handing SUN four large volumes)* You have a month, but earlier would be better. That should keep you busy while the Americans are here. *(Beat)* They come in, Sun, like a breeze in the middle of the night, blowing hot and cold, getting us stirred up, and then they'll sweep out of here and we'll be left. They'll send Christmas cards once a year and we'll be left. You need that job at the university. I need my job. I don't count on kindness of strangers.

(SUN stands, moves to get the book from on top of the desk. MEI YEN picks up the book.)

MEI YEN: I'll hold onto the Whitman.

(End of scene)

Scene Six

(Time: A few weeks later)

(Place: Friendship Store, filled with Chinese goods, only for foreigners. ELIZABETH and MEI YEN are at the counter.)

MEI YEN: Most Americans like to buy the silk pajamas at the Friendship Store. But wait for Shanghai for the leather jackets.

ELIZABETH: We're not silk pajama people. We're not leather jacket people either. We're quite sensible.

MEI YEN: Then maybe you should be frivolous. What a poor fate to be like a monk with an umbrella—no hair, no sky.

ELIZABETH: Mei Yen, not to be blunt—I'll be blunt. I didn't ask to come here. I was told "Be outside your hotel at two o'clock."

MEI YEN: You could have refused. They just do the plan to be polite. Everyone wants to go to the Friendship Store.

ELIZABETH: Okay, then, I'll buy something. *(To an unseen clerk)* That sweater. The peach colored one. How much is it?

MEI YEN: *(Whispering)* It's cashmere.

ELIZABETH: I'll take it. Charge. Do you take American Express?

MEI YEN: Don't you want to try it on?

ELIZABETH: No.

MEI YEN: Chinese sizes are smaller.

ELIZABETH: If it doesn't fit, I'll give it away.

MEI YEN: The thought's occurring that you're buying it to please *me*.

ELIZABETH: What if I am?

MEI YEN: Then you are acting in a typically correct manner for a Chinese person.

ELIZABETH: Then it may be the first time I'm doing anything right since I got here. *(Beat)* I'm not a "Goody Two Shoes" like Remy, or a lecturer in six languages like my husband. *(Beat)* What is it like to be alone? Sun said you live alone.

MEI YEN: Sun should mind her business.

ELIZABETH: No. I asked her.

MEI YEN: Sun has a loose mouth. The walls in China have ears. There are baby spies in every crack.

ELIZABETH: *What is it like?*

MEI YEN: What do you think?

ELIZABETH: Frightening.

MEI YEN: *(Shaking her head)* Powerful.

ELIZABETH: In America, for a time, everyone left their husbands.

MEI YEN: Here no one divorces. Only sometimes they get busy with work and disappear. And Sun's one to gossip! Her husband was in the U K for two years, and now he's leaving again. He came home to do his laundry.

ELIZABETH: I *believe* in practical arrangements. *(Beat)* Where were you in the Cultural Revolution?

MEI YEN: You're *very* forward.

ELIZABETH: I'm a doctor. I'm trained to ask questions.

MEI YEN: And I'm trained to evade them.

ELIZABETH: I studied ballet, but didn't have talent; so I went to medical school instead. And I'd like a favor. Could you persuade Comrade Wu to take me on a tour of your hospital?

MEI YEN: *(The two pick through the clothes, like any two women shopping)* Possibly Tuking Union.

ELIZABETH: Tuking Union's all American doctors. I want to observe the Chinese.

MEI YEN: There's no AIDS here. Just a few cases.

ELIZABETH: *(Skeptical)* So Comrade Wu explained.

MEI YEN: If you take no for an answer, that's appreciated. Professor Remy could learn from you. *(Beat)* Sun's mother, you know, was a dancer with the ballet in Beijing. In the Great Proletarian Revolution, they made her dance for hours with a corpse in the schoolyard, because she liked to dance, and made us watch. So, Sun for sure was one who denounced her own mother. She applauded after the dance.

ELIZABETH: They must have threatened her.

MEI YEN: Hey, the Gang of Four bullied everyone; but no one put strings on people's hands to make one clap against the other. Remy should be told to be cautious in her friendships.

ELIZABETH: No one tells Remy anything. Sun's even invited her home for dinner Sunday.

MEI YEN: But Wu takes us to the circus Sunday to see the famous tigers who jump through hoops. The seats were a last minute gift from your Ambassador, Mr Lord. You warn Professor Remy to stop stirring up winds. And Sun, of course, is unpredictable, a little *fangele*—crazy.

ELIZABETH: Is Sun's mother still alive?

MEI YEN: My God, no. She died while she was dancing with the dead person. Thirty-one hours. That's when Sun applauded. You call it a "dance marathon." Is that correct? *(Silence)* After, her father was in shock and they put him in a mental ward. When the G P R was over, he wanted to stay there. It was one of the only places where there still were flowers. He was a botanist. No more questions, except, what is "goody two shoes"?

ELIZABETH: It means "to be an excellent tap dancer."

MEI YEN: Like Fred Astaire.

ELIZABETH: Like Fred Astaire.

(End of scene)

Scene Seven

(Time: Mid-June, a Sunday afternoon)

(Place: Beihai Park, Beijing. SUN and REMY are in the park.)

SUN: This is how you play"fish." We both lie down on the grass like this.

(SUN lies down flat on her stomach. REMY follows.)

SUN: Then, we face each other, lying flat likes fishes, face to face.

(SUN and REMY arrange themselves face to face, lying flat on their stomachs, face to face)

SUN: Then we look at each other eye to eye. Then we tell what's in our heart. Fish never lie. We used to play this game...my girlfriends and I. We'd come to Beihai Park, like this, in front of the Bridge of Perfect Wisdom, in this spot near the lake, and so our ancestors couldn't hear us, we'd whisper.

REMY: *(Turning face up to the sun, then back again into the fish position)* Finally, a day off. They've been working us like dogs.

SUN: Tell me about it. Mei Yen gave me four American books to translate into Chinese, including *Bonfire of the Vanities*.

REMY: *Bonfire of the Vanities* is very long.

SUN: Yes, I know.

REMY: You should complain.

SUN: That's considered a bad attitude.

REMY: When do you have to finish?

SUN: In one month.

REMY: That's impossible.

SUN: *(Whispering)* No. Mei Yen wants to keep me busy while you're here. I think she's jealous. She's an independent woman, so she has no friends. *(Beat)* We may have to cancel when you're coming to my house. There could be no time.

REMY: Then we'll steal time. But we have to change the day. I'm expected at the circus Sunday. They got front row seats. I said I was invited to your house for dinner, but Mei Yen said "no".

SUN: Oh boy.

REMY: So another night.

SUN: Probably not; but you must see the amazing circus. The tigers are terrifying fun in the first row. One prays they don't mistake the audience for the hoop.

REMY: I thought you wanted to be friends.

SUN: Tell me a secret.

REMY: About what?

SUN: Anything no one else knows is a secret.

REMY: My brother taught me how to eat animal crackers. You eat the feet first, so you save the best part for last. He also taught me never to walk on yellow snow.

SUN: *(Considering it)* Never walk on yellow snow. *(Beat)* Now you say "fish."

REMY: Fish.

SUN: In Geneva, Switzerland I saw a young girl with golden hair sipping a lemonade the color of the sun. *(Beat)* Fish.

REMY: Once I stole perfume from a store. Fish.

SUN: When I shit in my pants when my mother died. *(Beat)* Who was the first boy to touch you? Fish.

REMY: Brian. He had blond hair and he put his hand on my blouse and squeezed my nipple hard. *(Beat)* Fish.

SUN: My cousin Chen Wei was home from the University and in the cool cellar, he put his fingers inside my shorts and touched my furry fuzzy. How could something that feels so good be so bad, so bourgeois? *(Beat)* Fish.

REMY: I'm not as strong as I look. *(Beat)* Fish.

SUN: A bicycle repair man makes more than a teacher. I want Ray Ban sunglasses like the boys who sell T shirts, and a tape machine and the lamps the tourists buy. I like beautiful jewelry. I have red eye disease. I don't want to stay up all night to read the American's books so I can return them in the morning, smile politely. "Thank you." Xie xie. "Would you care for a cup of tea?" (SUN *bows*) I want a job at the United Nations with an apartment and a window to look out and see the sky, like it was your own. *(Beat)* There are things I could kill for. *(Beat)* Fish. *(Silence)* Why do you eat the feet first on the crackers?

(REMY *hesitates, then—*)

REMY: So the animals won't run away.

(End of scene)

Scene Eight

(Time: A few days later. In the afternoon)

(Place: Tiananmen Square, Beijing. PHILIP and ELIZABETH are in a line to see Mao's glass cased tomb. ELIZABETH has on a red blouse. PHILIP, in sneakers, holds an official letter.)

ELIZABETH: I don't want to stand in this line. I don't want to see a dead person in a glass case.

PHILIP: Mao looks as good as new.

ELIZABETH: I want to go home.

PHILIP: The tickets can't be changed. There's a penalty.

ELIZABETH: I don't care.

PHILIP: Keep moving or someone will break into the line.

ELIZABETH: I'm not looking at the dead man.

PHILIP: We're in enough trouble. If you leave early, you'll disgrace us.

ELIZABETH: Wrong. They'll never let on. They'll be terribly polite and say they're so sorry my mother's sick.

PHILIP: How can your mother be sick? She's dead...God, Elizabeth, hang in there. It's only another four weeks.

ELIZABETH: *(Pointing to the sign)* Look at the sign—"Welcome" and "Keep Off Our Grass." *(Reading)* "Chinese admitted Mondays, Foreigners admitted Fridays. Decorous attire is encouraged—no shorts, sneakers, or bright colors." "Outsiders are still the barbarians. I'm wearing red, so we can't go in.

PHILIP: So I'm wearing sneakers. We've been in the damn line for an hour. We've got our permission letter. I'm staying.

ELIZABETH: Well I'm *not*. Ever since we got here, I keep ending up in places I don't want to be, like the Forbidden fucking City, or in this line to view the corpus delicti. I can't even get in to see a real hospital. *(Beat)* I called work and they're short-handed at the clinic.

PHILIP: Always.

ELIZABETH: That's not my fault! *(Beat)* I'll leave it to you and Remy to "*xie xie.*" Only keep an eye on "yours with a smile," Sun. I understand from Mei Yen she's slightly "*fangele*". *(Circling her finger)*

PHILIP: Mei Yen hates Sun.

ELIZABETH: Mei Yen doesn't like to be crossed. But hey, this is just the country where they kill the calligrapher if one letter of a word is wrong. That's too much pressure for me. I'll see you back at the hotel.

PHILIP: What am I supposed to tell Wu when he comes to pick us up?

ELIZABETH: That I went to the Friendship Store and I'll take a taxi home. I feel like buying a pair of pajamas. *(Starting to leave)* And my best to Chairman Mao. Tell him my favorite saying of his is "Enough of your farting." He forbid the people to fart. Some even died from holding it in.

(End of scene)

Scene Nine

(Time: The Next Morning)

(Place: Temple of the Sleeping Buddha, courtyard. COMRADE WU and PHILIP are talking.)

COMRADE WU: It's not allowed for the delegation to go anywhere alone. It's for protection.

PHILIP: It was Sunday. My wife was looking for a church.

COMRADE WU: There are no churches in China.

PHILIP: *(Taking in a deep breath)* Elizabeth may have to leave. She has an emergency at home. A relative is sick. Her mother is ill. Very ill.

COMRADE WU: Oh, I'm sorry. Was she ill before you left?

PHILIP: Probably. Yes. We aren't sure. She lives in Florida. *(Beat)* It's a place for old people. They like to go there because the sun shines and they do fun things. *(Beat)* Shit. She just wants to go home, Wu. She feels like an outsider here. She's outside the delegation and the delegation is on the outside of the inside. She wants to tour your P L A Hospital, but you won't take her.

COMRADE WU: I know.

PHILIP: How come you asked us here in the first place if you already know everything? *I* didn't hold back. I gave distinguished lectures. That's my job.

COMRADE WU: And this is mine.

PHILIP: You're a tour guide.

COMRADE WU: Exactly. In fact, I never would have toured Mongolia if it wasn't for my "re-education". I was married also. Now I'm a confirmed bachelor man. *(Pause)* But I don't want to get sentimental on you, Philip, about "the good old days." You know what they say about the good old days? They're mostly a product of bad memory.

(Pause)

I'll make arrangements for Elizabeth's perhaps sudden departure, and I know I speak for Mei Yen and the Government in sending our regrets for your mother-in-law's poor health. May she have an unusually speedy recovery. *(Pause)* We'll have the Embassy ensure your wife's safe arrival, but there's red tape, so be patient.

PHILIP: Can't you pull strings to get Elizabeth into the Army Hospital? I don't want her to leave. Being away alone can bring out the worst in people.

COMRADE WU: Or the sad bottom.

PHILIP: ... When the crusaders left for the Holy Land they had no idea where they were going and how they'd get there. It was a land like no other they'd seen, with sun and fruits on the trees, and it smelled of figs and honey and seemed like Paradise; and who could have imagined they would be, months later, one morning, standing knee deep in their own blood. They were as distant from home, they might as well have been on the moon.

(End of scene)

Scene Ten

(Time: Immediately following)

(Place: Classroom, Temple of the Sleeping Buddha. REMY and SUN at table facing D S, the class.)

REMY: "By the shore of Gitche Gumee
By the shining Big-Sea Water...

SUN: *(Interrupting)* One of the students would like to know...where *is* Gitche Gumee?

REMY: Longfellow tells us it's somewhere in the Northland.

SUN: *(Acknowledging a question)* Another student asks what your "take" is on the American Indian problem regarding the sale of Manhattan.

REMY: I believe the American Government is paying the Indians reparations. End of class. The class is over. The next class will cover Birds' Eye View, Modern American poetry.

(They exit, walking towards courtyard.)

REMY: The students seem more interested in the politics of America than the poetry.

SUN: You put a Kentucky Fried Chicken into the middle of Beijing, you're bound to make people curious.

(Pause)

REMY: I have a present for you.

SUN: You already gave me a present. The book.

REMY: No. This is the *official* present.

SUN: There's no need.

REMY: Yes there is. I *need* to give it.

(Thrusting a wrapped package into SUN's *hands.* SUN *hesitates.)*

SUN: The hope is that you didn't have so many "needs".

REMY: Open it! Come on, open it!

*(*SUN *opens the package reluctantly, painstakingly. She takes out a small box, opens it slowly, as though it were either a bomb or Pandora's box. She stares into the box. At first we don't know what's in there. She takes out the contents, holding up a long pearl necklace)*

SUN: Well, they're pearls.

REMY: Cultured pearls... *(Beat)* It means... *(Thinking of something, anything)* ...you conquered the Cultural Revolution.

(Silence)

SUN: It's difficult to accept these.

REMY: No. I want you to have them. It's okay.

SUN: Hold it! You don't know what's okay, Remy, so please don't tell me! *(Beat)* It would be easier not to take this gift. *(*SUN *hands back the pearls)*

REMY: I came here with too much. Please let me give you the pearls. It's our secret. My God, your country gave us two panda bears. They're right in the Washington Zoo.

*(*REMY *takes pearls and puts them on* SUN*)*

SUN: These are too important.

REMY: They're faux pearls. They're not valuable. *(Silence)* Well, do you like them? *(Silence)* I asked do you like them?

SUN: They're not valuable.

REMY: No, they're faux...fake.

SUN: I understand the translation. *(Beat)* It's not ingratitude. There *are* things I would want. If I get an advanced degree, I have a better chance for my promotion, so instead of a hundred twenty yuan a month—thirty-nine dollars and fifty cents American, I get a raise to a hundred eighty yuan. *(Beat)* I'm considered an intellectual, but I can't eat culture. And yes I like the pearls. I never had any. And it's the Japanese, of course, who are famous for their pearls.

REMY: Then I know what I could do.

SUN: Why do you have to *do* something? Why don't you volunteer in an orphanage?

REMY: Please don't patronize me. I want to recommend you to our department. You could come as a guest lecturer and get paid good money. I could find you a place to stay, or you can stay with us. I'm sending a letter.

SUN: If you write a letter, it could be found out and considered that I asked you for a favor, taking away your important time from teaching our students. For the same reason, I'm apprehensive about you coming to my house. *Don't. (Taking off the pearls)* And please, no offense, but take back the not valuable pearls.

(SUN *holds the pearls out, but* REMY *refuses to take them*)

REMY: I'm not taking them back, and you are not asking me to write the letter; it's my idea.

(Beat)

Want to play fish, Sun? Tell me a secret.

SUN: *(Hesitating)* I really like the pearls. Each one is different, cultured.... And Remy, a young actress in my Unit, plans to come to the States. Lili's twenty-two, and with the Youth Theatre. She doesn't speak English, but she's learning rapidly. She wants to be rich and famous. She's asked me, would you meet with her and tell her about New York? The only thing I know, I told her, the Bronx is up and the Battery is down.

(End of scene)

Scene Eleven

(Time: Three days later)

(Place: REMY's *hotel room, Beijing, Two chairs, a table, and a lamp.)*

PHILIP: Mei Yen told Elizabeth. Sun ratted on her mother, stood in the middle of People's Square and accused her mother of being a counter-revolutionary. Then they made the mother dance until she dropped dead and Sun laughed and clapped like a crazy person.

REMY: A lie I'm sure, or they beat her up.

PHILIP: Everyone was beat up. How do you think Mei Yen ended up in solitary for eight years? You better watch it with Sun. Once a rat, you don't turn into a pussy cat. She led the Red Guards on a guided tour through her house, straight to all the valuables. That's why she got an easy job out of town.

REMY: Mei Yen is just jealous Sun and I are friends.

PHILIP: No. Mei Yen is angry because Sun spent the Revolution cutting grass in the sun, and Mei Yen spent it in a stinking hole in the ground.

REMY: The Chinese were taught to obey authority.

PHILIP: So were the Germans.

REMY: And I wrote to the university inviting Professor Sun. She needs an advanced degree.

PHILIP: Are you crazy? Sun's some kind of a desperate nut. And we're being cut back on budget. How can you promise to add a foreigner?

REMY: I didn't promise.

PHILIP: She made you feel guilty.

REMY: She did not. She wants to come. I can tell. I sent them her resume. She's published. She's a well-known scholar!

PHILIP: *(Interrupting)* Has it ever occurred to you to want something and not go after it?

REMY: I wanted to do something for her.

PHILIP: Why?

REMY: I like to help.

PHILIP: Why?

REMY: It makes me feel good.

PHILIP: *(Grabbing* REMY's *arm)* It's not as free here as you think. You listen to me. I'm the Head. You're going to get us all murdered, chopped into chow mein.

REMY: *(Breaking free)* I understand this place, you know. I studied all year before we came. I read every history book about China. Everyone who ever took a ride down the Yellow River has written a journal and I've read it. Test me. Go ahead. *(Going on rapidly)* The Opium War, 1839-1842, the Taiping Rebellion, 1850-1864, the Sino-Japanese War 1894-95, 1908, the Empress Dowager dies, 1912, the child Emperor, Pu Yi, as seen in the movie *The Last Emperor*....

PHILIP: Enough!

REMY: *(The wind out of her sails)* If you don't mind, I'm expecting a guest, an actress friend of Sun's I've agreed to meet in my room. And yes, I have permission from the ministry. *(Pause)* And you don't know a damn thing about friendships. They have nothing to do with position.

PHILIP: They have *everything* to do with position. See you this afternoon at the Temple of Heaven. And take a hat to protect your head. It's supposed to be a scorcher. *(Beat)* This is not our country. We're just here for a shot. You're not Joan of Arc and I'm not Marco Polo. *(He exits.)*

REMY: (*Picking up phone*) Room 5. I'm expecting a Miss Lili Chan and a Miss Sun.

(*End of scene*)

Scene Twelve

(*Time: Immediately following*)

(*Place: Hotel lobby. LILI sits in a chair, on edge. SHERWOOD sits in the chair beside her, reading a Chinese newspaper. Note that the two same chairs can be used as in the previous scene. REMY enters.*)

REMY: Is there a Lili Chan here? I'm Remy. (*Going over to LILI, speaking slowly*) Are you Lili Chan?

LILI: (*Very excited*) Remy? Remy?

REMY: Lili?

(*The two embrace excitedly.*)

REMY: I was waiting for you in the room, but you didn't come up, so I didn't know what to do, so I came down. I don't know where Sun is.

LILI: (*Cutting into REMY's speech above, becoming simultaneous*) Wo bù zhidào Sun zài na li. Wo yi jing déng le yì gè zhang tóu le. (*I don't know where Sun is. I've been waiting for one hour. She's reliable. I don't understand.*)

(*During the above, SHERWOOD continues reading his paper.*)

REMY: Well what are we going to do? I don't speak Chinese, you don't speak English. (*Beat, slowly*) Do you speak English?

(*LILI looks at REMY perplexed. SHERWOOD puts down his paper.*)

SHERWOOD: (*To LILI*) Ni shuo Yingwen ma? (*Do you speak English?*)

LILI: Wo hui shuo yidian.

SHERWOOD: (*To REMY*) She speaks a little.

LILI: (*To REMY*) Good morning.

REMY: Ni hao.

(*The two woman nod approvingly, as though they've had a momentous communication*)

SHERWOOD: Excuse me. My name is Sherwood. I'm an Engineer and I'm here waiting for a group of Americans to arrive. I'm the translator for my company. (*Handing REMY and LILI each his business card*) I have a half hour before they come. I'd be happy to help you out. I'm a technical translator, you understand.

REMY: No, no, it's fine! Thank you! Xie xie! It's a miracle.
I'm an American Professor. I don't know where Professor Sun is. She's our translator. She's very punctual. This isn't like her. She's the one who asked me to have this meeting. This is Lili Chan. She's an actress.

SHERWOOD: *(Bowing)* Lili Chan! Oh my God! Miss Chan. I didn't recognize you. Usually in the films you play a peasant, or the one where you were in the army and had fallen on hard times. What an honor. I saw you in *The Old Well*. *(To* REMY*)* She won the Golden Rooster Award. It's like your Academy Awards. *(Excitedly)* This is one of the greatest days of my life! Lili Chan! *(To* LILI*) Wo hen rongxing. (Then, to* REMY*, translating)* I'm honored.

REMY: *(To* LILI*)* I understand you want to come to New York.

LILI: Hollywood.

REMY: This isn't easy.

LILI: Hollywood, exactly. Paul Newman, Robert Redford, Meryl Streep.

REMY: They're megastars, you know.

LILI: I know *that*. You know them?

REMY: No. *(Turning to* SHERWOOD*)* I think we should call Sun to see if she's okay. Could you ask Miss Chan if she has Sun's phone number...I have her address.

*(*SHERWOOD *whispers to* LILI, LILI *whispers back to him in Chinese)*

SHERWOOD: She doesn't have that information.

REMY: This is the address.

*(*REMY *takes out a piece of paper and hands it to* SHERWOOD*)*

SHERWOOD: *(Shaking his head)* This is just an address. It's complicated. Many people live in that block.

REMY: But this is where she lives.

SHERWOOD: Yes. In that block, somewhere. *(Shrugs)* Who knows? But if you want to speak with Miss Chan, you'd better hurry. I don't have a lot of time. So we'll begin. Miss Chan has many questions to ask you... *(Bending over, whispering with* LILI *in Chinese, then to* REMY*)* ...like what books or videos you brought... *(To* LILI*) Ni jinwan you kong ma, Xiaojie Chan? Xianzai qing kaishi .*

REMY: What did you say to her?

SHERWOOD: "Now please begin" ...and... *(Hesitating)* ..."Are you possibly free this evening, Miss Chan?"

(Lights down)

(End of scene)

Scene Thirteen

(Time: That same evening)

(Place: A street in Beijing. REMY, *paper and map in hand is wandering the street trying to find* SUN's *apartment house. It's raining.)*

REMY: *(Reading from the piece of paper)* Excuse me. Can you tell me where 25 Dongbin He Road is? Compound of the Ministry of Culture, Building 67, Entrance 5, Unit 2D? I'm looking for Sun Hong Tian. *(Silence)* Does anyone speak English? *(Looking in her Chinese dictionary) Duibuqi, ni hui shuo Yingwen ma? (Silence)* My translator is lost. *(Silence)* Oh shit.

(A man enters from the shadows. He holds an umbrella. We can not see his face.)

REMY: Excuse me... *Laojia...* Excuse me... *Laojia...* Hong Tian... Sun Hong Tian... I'm an American. I can't speak Chinese.... *(Looking in her dictionary) Wo bu hui shuo Zhongguohua...*I'm sorry...*baoquian...*

COMRADE WU: *(Only his voice, his face still hidden)* The people are afraid of *"baoquian"*.

REMY: *(Surprised)* Wu!

COMRADE WU: When the people saw they had misinformation about the Government, the offenders naturally wrote self criticisms, *"baoquians"* and then they were re-educated, *"laojiao,"* which means "excuse me." So, your words remind them of bitter times. But how could you know?

REMY: What are you doing here?

COMRADE WU: I could ask you the same question.

REMY: I'm looking for Sun. I have a letter for her. She didn't show up for a meeting.

COMRADE WU: Between you and the actress Lili Chan? You should have told me about that meeting. You said you were staying in to wash your hair.

REMY: I did wash my hair.

COMRADE WU: The others enjoyed the trip to the Temple of Heaven. They bought dozens of postcards. *(Silence)* It was explained if you wanted anything to ask me. Professor Sun, of course, is working for us, and you are our guest.

REMY: I can meet with somebody privately if I want to. The actress wanted some information on Los Angeles.

COMRADE WU: But that's not what you're here for.

REMY: What *am* I here for?

COMRADE WU: You tell *me*.

REMY: To get to know the Chinese better.

COMRADE WU: You won't.

REMY: For the Chinese to know us better.

COMRADE WU: They won't. That's not what they're after.

REMY: And what's that?

COMRADE WU: To take what's useful and spit the rest out. *(Beat)* Why did you come to our country?

REMY: You know why. To exchange cultures.

COMRADE WU: We invented culture.

REMY: It seems the Chinese invented everything.

COMRADE WU: You shouldn't have given Sun the pearls. It got her in trouble and makes you suspect *and* your small delegation.

REMY: *(Now frightened)* They weren't valuable, Comrade Wu.

COMRADE WU: Like the Whitman book? Sun, of course, reported the gift immediately.

REMY: If she reported it, what's the problem?

COMRADE WU: She shouldn't have accepted it. Questionable corruption.

REMY: Sun didn't want to take them. I insisted.

COMRADE WU: *(Angrily)* Well, that's not *our* problem. We're not a poor hungry pig-cow! Sun, of course, couldn't refuse. It would have been an insult to you. No Chinese would have refused. They'd rather die than humiliate.

REMY: Then it's not Sun's fault.

COMRADE WU: Look Miss Martin, you're a guest in China. Don't bite the hand of the Emperor. Sun will be at your next lecture.

REMY: I thought things were changed here.

COMRADE WU: They are. But you go back to New York; we get to stay.

REMY: I demand to know what's happened to her.

COMRADE WU: Home translating. There is a sudden demand now for all of William Faulkner's books...*The Sound And The Fury, Light in August. (Beat)* Did Sun share stories with you about the hard times in China?

REMY: She wasn't complaining.

COMRADE WU: Just passing information about current injustices to the outside world. That's a serious crime here. It loses face. *(Beat)* And it would be impossible to find Sun's apartment. Even I don't know where it is. If one wanted, one could go to the Public Security Bureau, but it takes weeks to get an appointment, and then, their files are *"nan"*—difficult. They will say

something like *"Zhongguo hen da"*—China is a very big place. *(Beat)*
Go home and leave Sun alone.

REMY: I *do* have some kind of conscience.

COMRADE WU: I don't care *what* you have. You can't tease her fantasies.
It will give Sun a twisted heart. There are few opportunities for us. You
don't need to teach us the "pioneering spirit." *(Beat)* Teach and go home.
Don't break your heart. Don't break ours. We're the ones who play Weiqi,
where you win by surrounding your opponent while he's trying to
surround you. This is a Chinese game and not for Americans.

(End of scene)

On The Great Wall

*(REMY and SUN advance clockwise on the wall to twelve o'clock, U S center and top
of the circle. They ascend very weary from the long climb.)*

SUN: The Middle Kingdom is the center of the earth, and China is the center
of that center. Everything there is in harmony and order. The rest is chaos.
(Pause) We're almost to the top.

(They stand looking over the edge)

REMY: Hyacinths and lilies and the wall goes on forever across the
mountains. There's a river and lotuses. Sun, look at this!

(They start to walk clockwise.)

SUN: Sometimes I think maybe Marco Polo never was to China, because
there's no mention of the Great Wall in his writing, and it was here when
he was here. And he was a student of architecture. If *he* wasn't here, maybe
it wasn't here. All of the west trying to come to Dongfang, the Orient, and
all the time, we're not even here, so you can't get to China.

REMY: At the beach, in the summer, I'd dig a hole, deep as I could, sure any
minute a dragon would leap from the sand, and I'd know I was there.

SUN: This year is The Year of the Dragon. It means a year of strength and
fire.

REMY: To The Year of the Dragon.

SUN: To the dragon, to the days of China's glory. *(Beat)* The Year of the
Dragon, its believed, is unlucky for travelers, so maybe I'll remain here
until next year. *(Beat)*

REMY: A letter came. It came this morning.

SUN: What did it say?

REMY: They want you. The University wants you. They want you to come.

(REMY and SUN start to walk clockwise down the wall, towards the place where they began. The lights fade.)

END OF ACT ONE

ACT TWO

Scene One

(Time: The next morning, sunrise)

(Place: Courtyard, Beihai Park. Early morning aerobics. Tango music is heard. The lights fade up slowly and we see three couples doing the tango—SHERWOOD and LILI, PHILIP and REMY, COMRADE WU and MEI YEN. Their movements are precise and perfect; they move swiftly, as if in a dream. The figures are lit so that they appear as silhouettes. After the beginning beats have been established, COMRADE WU, without missing a beat, changes partners, dancing with PHILIP, leaving REMY and MEI YEN. The two women, also without missing a beat, take on each other as partners, continuing to dance the tango. The music escalates in tempo. The lighting becomes brighter, as the sun rises higher. After a few minutes, PHILIP, changes partners, taking MEI YEN. REMY is left to dance with COMRADE WU. There should be a good deal of tension, as each changes, and the abandoned partner dances with the only choice, as in MEI YEN with REMY and REMY, finally, with COMRADE WU. Only SHERWOOD and LILI stay together for the entire scene, dancing closer and closer.)

(The music finishes. Lights slowly down. The dancers stop and the scene is in frieze.)

(End of scene)

Scene Two

(Time: Later the same day, close to noon. It is very hot.)

(Place: The Forbidden City, the courtyard in front of the Imperial Palace, Gate of Supreme Harmony. COMRADE WU stands encircled by MEI YEN, REMY, PHILIP, and ELIZABETH. All wear Chinese style bamboo lampshade hats. MEI YEN holds up a white umbrella, leading the group, as there are many tour groups in the vast courtyard of the Forbidden City.)

COMRADE WU: The Imperial Palace, also known as the Forbidden City, is located in the heart of Beijing, covers two hundred fifty acres, and is surrounded by a wall thirty five feet high. The complex contains over nine thousand rooms, which may soon be converted into hotel space for tourists.

MEI YEN: This courtyard could hold ninety thousand people during ceremonies.

ELIZABETH: I think we should move out of the direct sun.

COMRADE WU: *(Moving ahead)* We'll proceed now to the Hall of Supreme Harmony.

REMY: Where's Sun this morning?

MEI YEN: She has work.

COMRADE WU: It seems there's a Faulkner emergency.

REMY: *(Politely)* Begging your pardon, may I request a meeting with Sun? I haven't seen her and we have the next lecture to review. *(Silence)* If I can't meet with her, I'm unable to do my next class.

MEI YEN: Such arrogance. This could shock our students. Some of them have saved for over a year to come to the Summer Institute.

REMY: *(Under her breath)* I don't give a flying shit.

PHILIP: Cool it, Remy!

REMY: You cool it! Go eat a hotpot, Philip!

COMRADE WU: Sun has the flu.

MEI YEN: Sun hasn't the time for sight seeing.

REMY: *(To MEI YEN)* Because you're doing something with her.

MEI YEN: Sure. Chinese water torture.

REMY: I thought everything was so free here—1988, the new democracy. You throw up a Sheraton, but you tell a woman she can't have an American friend. And I don't want to see the Forbidden City. Probably a million people's bones are buried under here. I'm going back to the Hotel. I have the flu too. *(She starts to exit)*

COMRADE WU: You can't go to the hotel yourself. How will you get there?

REMY: By paying someone for the use of their bicycle. I plan to report Sun's disappearance to your police.

COMRADE WU: We have no police in China.

REMY: Who are the ones in the uniforms then?

COMRADE WU: In uniform? Hmm...traffic cops. Of course we have a Public Security Bureau, the P S B.

REMY: Then I'll tell the P S B, unless you want to tell me where she is.

MEI YEN: At her home.

REMY: It would be easier to find the Middle Kingdom than to find Sun's home.

COMRADE WU: The Middle Kingdom isn't a real place.

REMY: *That's* what I mean. It's impossible to locate. *(Turning to* MEI YEN*)* You're jealous because I gave Sun a book, because I gave her dumb jewelry!

MEI YEN: The pearls.

REMY: The pearls.

MEI YEN: Not jealous. Jealousy is wanting what someone else has. *(Beat)* Envy is wanting what someone else has and you don't want *them* to have it. I have envy. Maybe I want to play fish.

REMY: How do you know about fish?

MEI YEN: I also know how to be clear-headed. Be alone in a dungeon for one thousand days. I never let my guard down.

*(*REMY *exits.)*

MEI YEN: *(Pulling herself together, putting forward the public "face")* There's no concern. The P S B will assure Remy, Sun is safe and busy.

PHILIP: I apologize for my comrade's spirit.
And I apologize for my wife. She's not feeling well.

ELIZABETH: Dead wrong. I *am* feeling. I am absolutely feeling!

MEI YEN: *(Quickly, to cut off anymore emotional outburst)* In fact, Professor Sun tells me she is so taken with *The Sound And The Fury,* she doesn't sleep or eat and has even lost a stone of weight.

COMRADE WU: And now, this way to the Temple of One Hundred Buddhas, each in a different position. Though some call it "No Buddha Temple" since so many of the statues were "misplaced" during our Cultural Revolution.

*(*COMRADE WU *and* PHILIP *exit,* MEI YEN *and* ELIZABETH *linger behind in the courtyard.)*

ELIZABETH: *(To* MEI YEN*)* This morning I took a walk by Yuyuan Lake and everyone stared to see a westerner. *(Beat)* I'm changing my ticket and going back early. It has nothing to do with my mother. I have my work at home.

MEI YEN: How long have you been married?

ELIZABETH: Fifteen years.

MEI YEN: Do you love him?

ELIZABETH: Now *you're* being forward. Philip does the cooking, I do the bills, and we sleep together in the night. For Remy, it's different. She goes for passion.

MEI YEN: She's already separated.

ELIZABETH: *Quite* separated. *Left.* Adorable Remy wakes up one morning last month to find the cock has flown, so to speak, with her best friend. And not a whisper of a warning. She gave all his Armani suits away to Goodwill before she came to Beijing. *(Beat)* Remy loves China. There's so much missionary work here.

(End of scene)

On The Great Wall

(REMY and SUN walk very slowly now. The light is dimmer than before, as in late afternoon in summer. They walk towards six o'clock, now closer to where they began on the wall, D S center.)

REMY: So the Universe is China.

SUN: No. The *center* of the universe is China.
Everything else is away from the center.

REMY: Don't you consider that self-centered?

SUN: I never considered it.

REMY: And if you leave?

SUN: Only you can't, because it's in the center of you.

REMY: Then how will you come with me?

SUN: I would want to, and maybe have no choice.

REMY: But I made plans, wrote letters.

SUN: But I have a son here and a room, and every morning it's still uncertain which way the wind blows. We watch the sky like sailors.

REMY: If you don't come *now*, it may not happen. The University can change it's mind, bing-bang. You'll see. You'll love it—Radio City, Rockefeller Center. *(Adding)* I have a guest room. You could stay longer.*(Beat)* My husband is actually gone, gonzo, *fei,* flying, fly away *(Making the motion of a bird)* Like a bird.

SUN: *(Hearing, not hearing, Now circling D S on the circle)* Look, they're signaling! It's Philip! He's bought a T-shirt. It says "I CLIMB THE GREAT WALL". And Elizabeth's waving *her* purchase, a statue of a Chinese warrior. Wave back to Philip and Elizabeth. They're waving to us. *(Waving back)* Yoo hoo! We're coming!

REMY: *Ni hao ma!* Hello! *Ni hao ma!* Wait for us!

SUN: We're coming together. *(Beat)* It's strange that in other countries they study the Orient, but here in the Orient, we see no need to study ourselves; instead, our scholars go to Harvard and study with American Orientalists, and then come home and teach us ourselves reflected. *(Beat)* You know we invented gunpowder, but then the British came a thousand years later with

cannons, and everyone forgot we were the place where it began....
How can we be a third world country if we were the first?

(End of scene)

Scene Three

(Time: The next day, early morning)

(Place: P R C passport office, Beijing. SUN *is with the* PASSPORT OFFICER.*)*

PASSPORT OFFICER: Sun Hong Tian, you're applying for a passport?

SUN: To the U S for advanced study, so I can be a greater teacher,
sponsored by Professor Remy Martin, New York University.

PASSPORT OFFICER: Will you be selling or trading anything in America?

SUN: No, no, I want a J-1 Passport for professional work.

PASSPORT OFFICER: What Unit?

SUN: Beijing Institute of Foreign Languages, Literature Department.

PASSPORT OFFICER: *(Shaking his head)* I'm looking at my list here. No.
I don't see you under the list from your unit.

SUN: That's impossible. I'm with the Beijing unit.

PASSPORT OFFICER: It's *quite* possible. Let me see your papers.

*(*SUN *hands over her papers. The* PASSPORT OFFICER *looks them over,
then returns them.)*

PASSPORT OFFICER: You don't have enough papers. Please return in
two weeks with more papers and an application for B-2.

SUN: B-2! That's ridiculous! That's only for one month. That's for a
tradesman, not a teacher! What can I do in one month?

PASSPORT OFFICER: The passport is delayed.

SUN: I assure you I am a loyal member, sponsored by my Unit, approved to
go abroad for advanced degree, and opposed to bourgeois liberalization.

PASSPORT OFFICER *(Stamping her application)* Delayed. More research.
More papers. B-2.

(End of scene)

Scene Four

(Time: Later that same morning, the fourth of July.)

(Place: Temple of the Sleeping Buddha, classroom. MEI YEN stands in front of the class rather stiffly, clears her throat, and begins.)

MEI YEN: This is a puzzling situation. We have no idea where your professor is. She wasn't in her room this morning. As for your translator, Professor Sun has a reputation for being speedy on her *zixing che*, a daredevil on two wheels, so perhaps she has run into a road accident. And under our new free China, I worry about hooligans on the highway. Comrade Wu has gone to look for her. *(Beat)* Today is the Fourth of July which is a holiday of independence in the U.S. Perhaps Professor Remy is celebrating early. *(Beat)* Class dismissed. We'll meet tomorrow at Tiananmen Square for the kite flying competition.

(COMRADE WU comes running in followed by a much disheveled SUN on a bicycle.)

SUN: *Wo hen baoqian!* I was riding along, and a woman with a cart full of chickens came colliding into me with her bicycle, and then she was screaming at me and screaming at the running chickens. And then a truck came along and ran into the chickens, and they were then running around truly like chickens without their heads on, crashing into the man on the bicycle with cabbages. Smell me! Full of cabbage! *(Holding up the sleeve of her dress to MEI YEN) (Beat)* Where is Remy? *(Smoothing down her hair)* I am ready for my class.

MEI YEN: *(To the class)* Class will be over, please.

(Beat. MEI YEN waits for them to leave, then turns to SUN)

MEI YEN: You don't talk in front of the class like a wild monkey! And your professor has taken off and refused to teach. What a humiliation, and all because of your damned complaints, and how you failed to show up at our trip to the Forbidden City.

SUN: Begging your pardon, Mei Yen, but I had the translations to finish.

COMRADE WU: Your absence yesterday was disruptive. Unfortunately, it was not a successful outing.

SUN: Am I expected to do the work or tour the Forbidden City?

MEI YEN: Both. We're expected to show our faces.

SUN: Which face of our two faces?

COMRADE WU: I would be cautious with your rudeness, Sun.

SUN: Why? Is there a rat in this room?

MEI YEN: The superior man hesitates before condemning his neighbor's roof to be rotten.

SUN: Speak plain, Mei Yen.

MEI YEN: No one forgets what you did.

COMRADE WU: To your own parents.

SUN: *(To* COMRADE WU*)* So what your children did to *you*. It's all the same. We were made to be like refrigerators in that time. Open the door, close the door. Did you forgive your children, Wu? Then forgive me.

COMRADE WU: I don't even know their names anymore. Even my dreams are without their names.

SUN: I saw your son, Wu Yiding. He's well and has two children. He lives in Canton.

COMRADE WU: My ears aren't listening. *(Beat)* And what do you know about my not public only-ness?

SUN: Oh Wu, come on. You lick up the party line like a true shit!

COMRADE WU: My wife was a god-beautiful painter. *(Then angrily) Okay!* So, I was sleeping in my house, one morning, and she called me. "You hear the shouting? 'Down with Wu Xinguo, down with rightist Wu Xinguo.'" Then they brought me to the school where I was teaching and there were some student leaders, and my son with them, haranguing my crimes. My son joined the Red Guard and took on the name Li, Li the Faithful.

SUN: See. You do know his name.

MEI YEN: *(To* SUN*)* Don't invoke sentiment!

COMRADE WU: Excuse me, but I have an appointment at the Bureau to re-register for the Party. With my apologies, please go fly a kite in Tiananmen Square for Wu.

(COMRADE WU *exits.*)

MEI YEN: *(Making certain* COMRADE WU*'s gone)* Your American friend went to the Bureau to report you missing. Of course, I called them to correct the misinformation. We have to grease Wu's palms. We don't know where he stands. That's why I act like I do.

SUN: You gave me the work for spite.

MEI YEN: I gave you the work to keep you away from the Americans. You drool too much over them.

SUN: But I love the life of the scholar. I dream of the University, of going to Geneva as a translator, or maybe New York City.

MEI YEN: Remy is no ticket to a passport. She'll go home and you'll be forgotten, snow in a field of rice. Have some discipline! *(Calming herself, reciting, with accompanying Tai Chi movements) Hsu*—Patience and confidence will bring prosperity.

SUN: *(Frightened, but chiming in. This is a catechism-like recitation known to most educated Chinese, often recited during the C R.) Hsu* is a combination of water and Heaven.

MEI YEN: *(Still reciting,* SUN *joins in)* Without them everything would die. The sun is yang and the rain is yin. The earth needs light and water and we need help from those around us.

SUN: But Mao was crazy.

MEI YEN: You could be punished for that.

SUN: You still think I'm a traitor because I acted with the rest of the young Red Guards.

MEI YEN: You have no idea *what* I'm thinking.

SUN: *Baotai.*

MEI YEN: No! No *Baotai. (Banging her hand against her forehead) Kong! Kong! Kong!* Empty! *(Softly)* I can't remember how to have an original thought. *(Beat)* You turned on your mother. You could do the same to me. You might even clap.

SUN: *(Angrily)* I clapped so she could hear me while she danced! *(Beat)* I want to go to New York, but I need more papers—a permission letter from you. Please. My heart is leaping to get my advanced degree. And not selfish, but to soak it in, then bring it back here so we aren't dumb Asians. Professor Remy has absolute permission in a letter. How can I humiliate the American offer? I have been popular, obedient, and even dreamed once of being in love with Mao and knitting him a sweater, which proves my loyalty. My son will stay with strict relatives, and then I'll come home, Mei Yen. I was just crazed before. Afterwards, when the clapping was over, I even twisted the head of a rooster. Since then, everything has been in a straight line.

MEI YEN: Perhaps you were crazed in those years.

SUN: I was crazed. Let me go. I promise I'll come home. *(Beat)* I was crazed.

(Lights down)

(End of scene)

Scene Five

(Time: The next afternoon)

(Place: Tiananmen Square. SHERWOOD, LILI, PHILIP, ELIZABETH, MEI YEN, REMY, *and* SUN *are scattered in the Square, flying colorful kites, some in the shapes of animals, some with musical instruments on them that whistle in the wind.)*

REMY: *(Moving closer to* SUN, *in a whisper)* I thought you'd been murdered.

SUN: *(With no emotion)* My position requires many hours of work. I'm happy to do what's asked of me. Our goal is to educate the students in official policy.

REMY: *(Whispering)* I even went to the Security Bureau to report you missing.

(Silence, as SUN *takes this in)*

REMY: But they were closed for lunch, open again at three. So I went back at three, but there were lines around the block. When I went back at four, they said it was closed for a special meeting, "No more appointments." And then it was just closed.

SUN: The Security officials are hard workers and vigilant defenders of our government and thought reform. Their paperwork is heavy. *(Whispering)* You didn't say my name?

REMY: *(Whispering)* I didn't get that far.

SUN: *(Whispering)* Never do that again. It could put me on the "hit list".

REMY: *(Softly)* I have more information. The visiting fellowship is for one year. They said "Yes! Good! We encourage multi-cultural!" You'll teach, even get faculty housing, and can take all the classes you want *free*.

(The others come closer)

SUN: The sky is Ming blue today.

MEI YEN: *(Moving closer to them)* The wind is brisk northwest, a good sign for kite flying.

SHERWOOD: If it were raining, that's the best luck.

SUN: The kites are an offering to Heaven, telling the gods we're here and to have pity.

MEI YEN: The prize is, the one whose kite stays up the longest gets to live the longest.

ELIZABETH: *(Having trouble keeping her kite aloft)* A questionable trophy.

MEI YEN: Long life is good fate. That's why such a crowd is out today, hoping.

SHERWOOD: I can't tell you the last time I took a summer day off just for pleasure. I have Lili to thank. She is such an opportunist.

LILI: Sherwood is like all scientists—work, work, work.

SHERWOOD: What about last weekend? Lili is such a party butterfly. We went to the Jingjiang Club in Shanghai, and sat in the first row.

LILI: And were lucky the topless dancers didn't jump into our laps. Sherwood thought it was funny. *(Playfully nudging* SHERWOOD*)* Didn't you, Xuehua. *(His Chinese name, meaning "snowy birch tree.")*

(Accidentally, LILI knocks his kite down)

SHERWOOD: Oh, no. Lili! Look what you did! You knocked down my kite!

LILI: It was a mistake.

MEI YEN: Sherwood is *out.*

LILI: *(To SHERWOOD)* I'm sorry. I was only being a playful kitten.

SHERWOOD: I have to go back to work anyway. *(To LILI)* Next time, be more careful. How will you be such a great actress if you make other people fall off the stage? *(SHERWOOD exits.)*

ELIZABETH: This is the perfect outing for my last day here. A lovely diversion before it's back to the wars. *(Moving closer to REMY, away from the others)*

REMY: *(Sarcastically)* Thanks for running home.

ELIZABETH: *(Sticking close to REMY, whispering)* The heat's oppressive, the government's oppressive, the bathroom's like a rice paddy, and the food is nothing like Chinese food. Why should I stay? I have nothing to prove.

REMY: And I do?

ELIZABETH: That you can fix everything. That's supposed to be *my* job. *(Struggling harder with the kite to keep it from falling)*

REMY: You don't think I'm playing with fire?

ELIZABETH: *(Moving towards the rest of the group)* Oh I do.

(ELIZABETH's kite finally falls.)

ELIZABETH: Maybe if I stayed another few weeks, I might really understand China.

PHILIP: *(Now struggling to keep his kite up)* Come on! Stay up there! I'm not letting go!

LILI: That Sherwood is such a foolish boy. He has too much pride.

ELIZABETH: He's in love with you.

LILI: *(Letting go of her kite)* How do you know?

ELIZABETH: *(As she exits)* I watched him watching you.

(LILI exits.)

MEI YEN: The wind's changed to the south. We should move to the foot of the Peace Gate, near Mao's portrait. If the breeze dies down, it's more favorable in that spot.

(MEI YEN exits, followed by PHILIP. SUN and REMY remain, their kites still up and just the music of their two kites.)

REMY: *(Whispering)* Are you okay?

SUN: *(Beat, whispering to* REMY) When would the job begin?

REMY: As soon as you get your passport.

(End of scene)

Scene Six

(Time: Afternoon, several days later)

(Place: Tea room, Beijing. REMY *and* SUN *have tea.)*

REMY: Fish.

SUN: No fishing today.

REMY: What about the passport?

SUN: Still delayed.

REMY: Why?

SUN: Complex. I brought them the more papers and permission from Mei Yen. I go back in one week.

REMY: In a week *(Flying motion, like a bird)* free as a bird.

SUN: If you were my sister, my mother, I would come and be roommates. Do you have grass in Central Park or just murderers?

REMY: This is a quite vicious rumor that we have only murderers.

SUN: We kids were all asked to join the Red Guard and Sun was shipped off to Binyang in the South to cut grass. Our quota was three hundred catties of grass a day. I spit at grass.

REMY: When your mother danced and died...

SUN: Correct...

REMY: And you clapped...

SUN: Correct...

REMY: So...

SUN: So...

REMY: What kind of person does that make you?

SUN: What kind?... Somebody says one day blue is dangerous, and lists the reasons, which seem logical. So you throw out all the blue. The next year, they say blue is good, and the arguments for that are just as logical. So then you reconsider. Maybe the blue wasn't so bad. *(Beat)* I clapped so she could hear me. *(Starting to clap—clap, clap, clap)* I'm sorry. *(Clap, clap, clap)* I love you *(Clapping faster and faster—(Clap, clap, clap)*I'm sorry. *(Clap, clap, clap)* I love you *(Clap, clap, clap)* I'm sorry. *(Clap, clap, clap)* I love you

(SUN, *then seeing* LILI *and* MEI YEN *enter the tea room, changes the subject rapidly.*)

SUN: *(To* REMY*)* ...So, a B-2! That's for a noodle salesman, I told him.

MEI YEN: *(Now in the tea room, to* SUN*)* Maybe the Passport Officer was given a "small report." *(Explaining to* REMY*)* We call this a "little report". There are watchdogs around with soft ears who hear gossip and report it. It could be your best friend. *(Passing plate of cookies)* Almond cookies make you happy. Everyone take one, please. This is a real girl-party.

REMY: Comrade Wu. Maybe he's a watchdog. He followed me when I was looking for Sun.

SUN: When?

REMY: When you didn't show up at my hotel. *(Beat)* You didn't come to the tour of the Forbidden City either.

MEI YEN: Perhaps now I think Sun saw plenty of the Forbidden City when the Red Guard was stationed there.

LILI: She brought the best sweet rice pudding every Sunday to her husband and the rest of us. We gobbled it like turkeys. Her husband was a great supporter of the arts. He encouraged my acting career.

SUN: He encouraged *numerous* actresses.

LILI: He put me in charge of the "free workers" theatricals. Now, when I go to the U S, I plan to dedicate my first performance to Comrade Sun.

MEI YEN: To the U S? But what about Sherwood? What are you, Lili? A western woman, about to choose a career over love?

LILI: Oh, Sherwood is applying to U C L A for graduate work. He's smart and one hot guy. We plan to live in Los Angeles. Oranges grow on trees there. First we have to get our passports. There are quotas. One has to move quickly to the front of the line.

SUN: They're in a violent mood at the Passport Office. Questions, more questions, new rules, blah, blah, blah. You should be prepared.

LILI: No problem. I have comrades in that office. *(Turning to* SUN*)* And if you come to the U S next year, Sun, maybe we'll meet in the Central Park.

MEI YEN: Am I to be the last Chinese left in Beijing? Lili is love struck, and Sun can't wait to leave, like a frog about to swallow the moon.

REMY: My university has invited Sun.

SUN: If I get the passport.

REMY: They can't refuse, or we'll get the students to write and say what a great teacher she is, what an honor to China she is.

LILI: This is not the sixties. You have a wrong attitude.
The government doesn't listen to students.

REMY: *(Frustrated)* What do they listen to?

MEI YEN: Flattery.

LILI: *(Shaking her head "No") Bribery.* I know those officials. Some of them
were in my old Unit. As for myself, of course, I'm not concerned, because
my history is clear.

SUN: Is that supposed to mean mine is cloudy? To this day I could recite
a self criticism with such conviction, you would swear it was true. I could
flatter the face of a mongoose without blinking an eye. Isn't that proof Sun
Hong Tian is re-educated, therefore suitable for passport? Only once was
I put under house arrest, because I complained for a hat in the summer.
I was told I was insolent.

MEI YEN: You sometimes are.

SUN: True. I then expressed deep sorrow to the Guards for my "erroneous
views," to show my Party spirit. What a splendid liar I became. *(Beat)*
There are things I could kill for.

REMY: You were brave, Sun.

SUN: No. All the brave ones are dead.

(End of scene)

Scene Seven & Scene Eight

(Time: Three days later)

*(Scene Seven Place: Hotel room, Shanghai. SHERWOOD and LILI in bed. Scene
Eight Place: Classroom, Temple of the Sleeping Buddha. REMY is finishing her
lecture D S. SUN translates.)*

(Note: Scenes Seven and Eight are performed intercut, as indicated on S R and S L.)

(Scene Seven)

SHERWOOD: Did your meeting go well?

LILI: *(Tracing her finger around the moons of SHERWOOD's finger nails, one by
one)* It always goes well in Shanghai. They served French champagne at
lunch and escargot. But then it was a little spoiled by some rotten apples
who shouted rude slogans outside on Nanjing Road. These dissidents,
they ruin it for the rest of us and are to blame for all China's troubles.
It puts me in bad humor. Tell me a story...

(Scene Eight)

REMY: Robert Penn Warren is known for his poetry and novel "All The King's Men," taken from the Mother Goose rhyme, Humpty Dumpty.

(Scene Seven)

LILI: ...a bedtime story. I'll close my eyes. *(She does)*

(Scene Eight)

REMY/SUN: *(Simultaneous translation)*
Humpty Dumpty sat on a wall,
Humpty Dumpty had a great fall,
All the king's horses and all the king's men
Couldn't put Humpty Dumpty together again.

Han pu di, dang pu di, zai giang shang zuo
Han pu di, dang pu di, zai le ge,
Suo you guo wang, de ma he suo you guo wang di ren
Duo bu len be Han pu di dang pu di chong zu he.

REMY: And the final poem, by that curmudgeon, Robert Frost.

SUN: *Zui hou yi shou shi, zuo zhe lin se gui Luo bo te Fu luo si te*

(Scene Seven)

SHERWOOD: My parents named me "*Xuehua.*" "*Xue*" is snow, and "*hua*" is birch tree, and Sherwood is like forest.

(Scene Eight)

REMY/SUN: *(Simultaneous translation)*
"The Oven Bird"

"There is a singer everyone has heard,
Loud, a mid-summer and mid-wood bird,

(Scene Seven)

SHERWOOD: When I was born, at the beginning of the Cultural Revolution, my parents were sent to the Russian border, near Lake Xingkai.

(Scene Eight)

REMY/SUN: *(Simultaneous translation)*
The bird would cease and be as other birds
But that he knows in singing, not to sing.

(Scene Seven)

SHERWOOD: There was only snow and birch trees covering the earth there.

(Scene Eight)

REMY/SUN: *(Simultaneous translation)*
The question that he frames in all but words
Is what to make of a diminished thing."

(Scene Seven)

SHERWOOD: They wanted the name "Xuehua" for me, to remember I was born in the difficult times. *(Beat)* Are you asleep?

(Scene Eight)

REMY: Some say Frost was speaking of sex; others, that he was predicting the fall of America.

(Scene Seven)

LILI: No, no. I'm listening, but the sound of your voice makes me sleepy—nice.

SHERWOOD: Are you going to fall asleep before we make love?

LILI: No. Just after.

(Scene Eight)

SUN: Our farewell banquet will be at the Sick Duck Restaurant, a week from today. At that time we'll say "zai jian"—goodbye.

(Lights fade)

(End of Scene Eight)

(Scene Seven)

SHERWOOD: Out of politeness, I'm asking if this is the first time.

LILI: In Shanghai, it is the first time, brother.

SHERWOOD: Then do you prefer the lights out?

LILI: No—*on.* I like to see. I like to compare.

SHERWOOD: *(Embracing her)* Naughty girl. Compare to whom?

LILI: I have practice saying bad things like this because of my experience in the theater.

SHERWOOD: Then how will I know who is you and who is the character you're playing?

LILI: Come inside and find out... But first, woo me.

SHERWOOD: *(He begins)* Once upon a time...Tang Qi was a poet and my friend....

LILI: Tang Qi was a famous dissident.

SHERWOOD: *(Correcting her)* Lili, he was a famous hero. *(Then reciting)* "Dawn and our train will soon arrive *(He kisses her.)* Blue light *(Kissing her again)* Pure white snow *(And again)* Countless hearts, a long chain *(Kissing her once more)* Marches into the forest..." *(Again. Beat)* You're asleep.

LILI: No, dreaming. Dreaming of you, and how in the morning, I'll wake up first, and you'll be lying on the white sheets, still dreaming of me, and how it was to be on the inside of me.

(End of Scene Seven)

Scene Nine

(Time: Later that week, late July.)

(Place: The Ming tombs, Xian. COMRADE WU, LILI *and* PHILIP *[camera slung over his shoulder] stand inside a large dimly lit tomb, viewing the 80,000 life size terra cotta warriors buried with the First Emperor.)*

COMRADE WU: The eighty thousand life size terra cotta warriors in this underground tomb, were discovered in Xian when a group of peasants were digging a well. It's estimated that forty thousand more clay warriors and horses are still buried here. The Emperor didn't want to be lonely in Heaven.

*(*PHILIP *snaps a photo of the terra cotta warriors)*

LILI: *(Grabbing* PHILIP's *camera from him)* NO CAMERAS, PLEASE!

COMRADE WU: *(Grabbing the camera from* LILI, *putting it into his knapsack quickly)* Do you want to get us arrested? Didn't you see the "obey" sign, Philip? NO CAMERAS.

LILI: *(To* COMRADE WU) *Mao zou le.*

PHILIP: *(To* COMRADE WU) What did she say?

COMRADE WU: "The cat is gone out of the bag." You've made trouble. They see us. The Guards are discussing it.

PHILIP: I wanted to take a photo to show Remy.

LILI: Yes, it's a shame she was sick and couldn't come. This is our major tourist sight. We're honored to be in the presence of such important history. My patriotic feelings here make me close to tears.

*(*MEI YEN *enters)*

MEI YEN: The good news is our entrance fee is waived. One of the guards has seen Lili on television and also knew her from the Youth League.... The bad news is that they want Philip's camera.

*(*COMRADE WU *takes camera out of his bag and quickly hands it over to* MEI YEN)

COMRADE WU: *(Frightened, to* MEI YEN) Did they see me put the camera in my bag?

MEI YEN: It's okay. They said they know Lili.

PHILIP: *(Grabbing the camera back)* It's not okay. They can't have my camera.

LILI: They give it back.

PHILIP: Sure, two weeks from now, like the *New York Review of Books*, when I'm in an airplane over the Atlantic.

MEI YEN: *(Taking the camera back)* Let me have the camera, Philip. I'll wait outside. I'll call the hotel and see how Remy is, poor girl, lying in her room with the Beijing flu.

LILI: And how Sun is making out at the Passport Office. Sherwood had no trouble this week when he showed the "Yes" letter from U C L A. And I meant to say earlier, Philip, how sorry I was that Elizabeth had to depart so speedily because of her sick mother. How *is* her mother?

PHILIP: Better.

LILI: American women seem so sensitive. At least that's the impression I get from reading *Vogue* magazine. *(Beat)* Mei Yen and I will wait outside. The breath of too many people in here at one time can destroy the art.

(LILI and MEI YEN exit.)

COMRADE WU: *(To PHILIP)* Is your wife's mother truly ill?

PHILIP: Of course not.

COMRADE WU: I didn't think so.

PHILIP: My wife and I aren't in love anymore and we don't know why.

COMRADE WU: My wife was an artist. But now I'm night-lonely.

PHILIP: I know. I think about women. That Lili is one hot pistol.

COMRADE WU: Keep away from Lili. She's taken.

PHILIP: Oh Sherwood's just a kid.

COMRADE WU: *(Looking around to make sure no one is watching them)* No. Not Sherwood. Someone high up in the party, with "guan-xi," with connections.

PHILIP: If she wants to be an actress, she'll need plenty of "guan-xi."

COMRADE WU: *(In a whisper)* Lili's not always an actress. She just acts like an actress. *(Shrugs)* China is a plate of sand. I'm sorry. A saying for everything.

PHILIP: But aren't *you* high up in the party? One night you followed Remy in the street.

COMRADE WU: Small cabbages. I used to be something, but I'm nothing now. I act like a cadre, but my only morality is survival. *(Beat)* I think about women also, Phillip. I have a part of a book. An old pal had three chapters he hid away and they never found it in his home when they looted it... *Lady Chatterly's Lover...Whew!*

PHILIP: When I get home, I'll send you the rest of the chapters. I have them in my house.

COMRADE WU: It's okay, Philip. I like the first three chapters very much.

(End of scene)

Scene Ten

(Time: The same day)

(Place: Passport Office, Beijing. SUN sits silently, stiffly, clearly terrified. The PASSPORT OFFICER enters with stack of papers. SUN stands.)

PASSPORT OFFICER: *(Dismissing SUN with a wave, sitting down, taking his time going through the papers. SUN waits, then finally he begins)* We would like to say "Yes, approved, no problem, *wenti*", but Sun Hong Tian...

SUN: But...

PASSPORT OFFICER: You are so special and valuable, so needed here. How can we let you leave? Your translating skills are too important. In fact, there's a possibility you'll be transferred...let me see here.... *(Looking through his papers)* Yes, here it is... *(Studying the piece of paper)* A position in the First High School in Gansu Province.

SUN: Gansu! That's practically in Tibet. I'm a university Professor, not a High School teacher. I've done nothing wrong.

PASSPORT OFFICER: *(Accusingly)* It isn't good enough for you *here*! It's good enough for the rest of us! You have a swollen head, Sun Hong Tian.

(REMY enters. SUN doesn't see her at first. PASSPORT OFFICER to REMY)

PASSPORT OFFICER: Excuse me. Yes?

SUN: *(Turning around, panicked)* Remy! What are you doing here?

REMY: I have the list. The students just finished signing their names saying how valuable a teacher you are.

PASSPORT OFFICER: What list? Let me see this list. *(To SUN)* Who is this person?

SUN: *(To PASSPORT OFFICER)* She's an American Professor and my visiting friend. I'm her official translator.

PASSPORT OFFICER: *(To REMY)* You have no business here. *(Pointing to SUN)* Even *she* has no business here.

REMY: But I have an official letter of invitation from my university. *(Handing him the envelope)* Here. Look.

PASSPORT OFFICER: *(Opening the envelope, scrutinizing the letter and the list of students as he speaks)* The students on this list are also questionable, well known as dissidents. And if our Sun is so valuable, how can we let her go? *(Closing his file, standing, as though the meeting is over)*

REMY: But I have a very good job for her in the United States.

SUN: *(Turning to the* PASSPORT OFFICER*)* I'm telling you, I have nothing but my country in my heart.

PASSPORT OFFICER: You have yourself in your heart.

SUN: *(Very angry now, To the* PASSPORT OFFICER*)* What do you know? You know nothing! You're just a machine doing paperwork, stupid work. You know nothing about me!

PASSPORT OFFICER: Shut up foolish woman! I know plenty! *(Waving the papers)* Conspiring with foreigners, stirring up the students, trying to bribe an official...

SUN: That's not true! I did everything right! I did just what you asked! I filled out all the forms, I learned every song *(Singing, with increasing intensity and loudness) Dong fay hóng tài yang sheng Zhòrg gúo chule yige Mao Tse Tung Chule. (The East is Red, The Sun Rises..../China has a Mao Tse-Tung/ He finds happiness for the people/He's the Great Savior of the people....)* *(Continuing at a fevered pitch)* I joined the Thought Reform Movement. I even clapped for my mother while she danced to her death, I named every villager, I gave directions to their houses!

PASSPORT OFFICER: Everyone knows how you incriminated your mother and father, confessed lies rather than be shot. Who would be stupid enough to trust you now?

REMY: You told her, her parents were bad, in the Cultural Revolution.

PASSPORT OFFICER: The American Professor recites our history to us. *(Beat)* This is *my* table, *my* office. *(To* REMY*)* Your passport.

REMY: I don't have it with me.

PASSPORT OFFICER: Always carry your papers, I D.

SUN: They're at her hotel.

PASSPORT OFFICER: *(Paying no attention to* SUN, *directly to* REMY*)* Your papers please, delivered here today.

SUN: Yes, sir, delivered promptly. We both respect your good judgment and approval for exit.

REMY: *(To* PASSPORT OFFICER, *realizing they both are in trouble)* Give me my letter back, please.

(The PASSPORT OFFICER *remains motionless.)*

REMY: Maybe she could come next year, if Sun is needed here that badly,

SUN: That's a lie!

PASSPORT OFFICER: Shut up your Chinese face. The purpose of the teacher is to reverse the thinking of the students.

SUN: *(Furiously to the* PASSPORT OFFICER*) Wo cao ni ma! (Chinese translation)* Bastard!

PASSPORT OFFICER: For that obscenity I spit in your face.

(He spits at SUN. *She just stands there. He slaps* SUN*'s face. She doesn't move. This is not the first time she's been slapped.)*

REMY: *(Frightened)* There's no job! It's a mistake! Someone else applied first. Give me my letter. No job. Sun stays here. No room in my apartment anyway. Filled with cockroaches. I only have one bedroom. I want to live alone. I need my privacy.

SUN: *(To* REMY*)* Traitor. Two-faced visiting friend. Why did you start up with me? I'm happy here. I have a fine life, everything a girl could want....

PASSPORT OFFICER: *(To* SUN*)* Quiet, you. *(To* REMY*)* You leave. *Zou!* I D papers here today.

REMY: *Xie xie. (She exits.)*

PASSPORT OFFICER: *(Pulls the pearls out of his pocket, the same ones* REMY *had given* SUN*)* And what are these?

SUN: Those are my pearls.

PASSPORT OFFICER: Then how did I get them? *(To* SUN*)* Who is Mei Yen.

SUN: My superior.

PASSPORT OFFICER: Tell your superior she's dumb. It would take more than pearls. *(Beat)* This meeting is over. *(Standing)* You should start packing your bags for Gansu, Sun Hong Tian, and don't forget your boots. There's much rain there. *(Then, holding out the pearls)* Here, take them. Go ahead. Take them back.

(No one moves, then)

SUN: *(Grabbing the pearls from the* PASSPORT OFFICER*)* The pearls are *not even valuable!*

(As SUN *grabs the pearls from him and starts to hit him with the pearls.)*

PASSPORT OFFICER: You'll be punished for this Sun Hong Tien!

(Blackout)

(End of scene)

Scene Eleven

(Time: Several hours later)

(Place: Public Security Bureau, detention room, Beijing. SUN and REMY are separated by a screen. They talk through the screen.)

SUN: They hold me here for a day. Questions, more questions.

REMY: The guard said "kuai wu". He shouted.

SUN: This is Beijing Detention House, not Central Park.
Five minutes quickly and don't come again.

REMY: The Passport Officer sent me here. He said it was okay.

SUN: Ha! Lili said it was okay to give pearls for a bribe.
I trust no one.

REMY: I brought you rolls.

SUN: Thank you, I've been fed. *(Beat)* Do you know where Gansu is?

(REMY shakes her head "No" on the other side of the screen, not answering)

SUN: The end of the world. The Yellow River crosses the Great Wall there, and the winds from the Gobi desert blow cold in your face. Why did you lead me on? Pursue Sun like a pet to bring home in your sleeve? *(Not waiting)* I asked you for nothing! *(Recalling REMY's earlier speech)* "We hope our small delegation can share our American spirit, our pioneering spirit." What does that mean, "pioneer"? I looked it up—"To colonize, ride in and take over land, annex it, make it yours." I had the good life before you came.

REMY: That's a lie. *(Starts to eat the rolls, slowly at first, then frantically)*

SUN: If it is, then it's the lie I choose.

REMY: Sun, we're friends, like sisters ...Fish...

SUN: You must have been mistaken. You exaggerate some friendship between us. We are acres apart. I invite you to my house, but I'm just being polite to a visitor. You know us Chinese. *(Beat)* And the Whitman. *Xie Xie.* I'm finished. *(Taking the Whitman book out of her bag and pushing it under the screen out to REMY)* As I'll be traveling, it's important to lighten the load.

(REMY accepts the book, holding it, as though it weighed a hundred pounds.)

(Lights fade.)

(End of scene)

Scene Twelve

(Time: A few days later. The first of August. It is late at night.)

(Place: Hotel room in Beijing. REMY sits very still, in a large overstuffed chair. White crocheted doilies are on each arm of the chair. The only illumination is from a small lamp. After a minute, she gets up, puts on a small tape recorder. American music. The sound of a knock at the door.)

REMY: Who is it?

MEI YEN: *(O S. In a whisper)* Mei Yen.

(Lights up more fully as MEI YEN enters the room.)

MEI YEN: Is it too late?

REMY: *(Staring straight ahead)* What time is it?

MEI YEN: Past eleven.

REMY: It's okay.

MEI YEN: There's all this paper work, closing the Summer Institute. *(Silence)* The students were sad. This is the first year we didn't have a farewell banquet. Last year the Americans sang "Yankee Doodle Dandy", and also, "I'd Like To Get You On A Small Boat To China", and everyone danced. *(Silence)* I saw Philip downstairs in the bar.

REMY: Philip likes to drink.

MEI YEN: I'm sorry about the pearls. I did it with good intentions for Sun. Lili insisted it would be an excellent bribe. She even offered to bring the pearls personally to the Officer. It was, now it seems, careless.

REMY: Lili—the actress who isn't really an actress.

MEI YEN: Also, as it seems, she was lying.

REMY: Oh, Christ, Mei Yen! Lili is an actress, but not, and Comrade Wu is loyal, but isn't, and Philip is together, but he's not, and you honor your mother, but spit at other women because you have red envy, and Sun spits at her mother's grave because she's loyal to the Government, but then the Government screws *her*, or Lili screws her, or I screw her, or she screws herself.

MEI YEN: The meaning of "screw", please.

REMY: We sometimes use it to mean "making love." Also, it's like being a rat; doing someone in. *(Beat)* I was stupid. I got Sun wanting.

MEI YEN: Sun was already wanting. We never know here what one thing it is which makes the Government irritated. It could be Sun only ate noodles in the wrong shop.

REMY: I wish I hadn't come.

MEI YEN: Except you did. When Marco Polo came to China, our land extended from the Yellow Sea to the Mediterranean, from Siberia to India. China was the jewel in the Empire. Marco Polo passed through cities of such greatness, even he was astonished. *(Beat)* Sun is a lucky one. She still knows her own heart. Mao warned that people are not like leeks. If you cut off their heads, they don't grow back.

REMY: It's possible she planned to kill herself if they didn't give her the passport.

MEI YEN: Perhaps. Comrade Wu tells me she's now in Prison No. 1 and that's all we know. She may have a trial. Maybe not.

REMY: I should see her. I should apologize. *(Knowing what a mess she's made of it)* I should tell her in High School I was voted "The Girl With the Most School Spirit." *(Silence)* I should do nothing for once.

MEI YEN: Sun knows you're her friend. *(Beat)* So, she is perhaps in solitary.... Yes, she's in solitary, Wu said. So she is alone, but possibly dreaming. We're used to "Hsu", patience, and just consuming time. Time is the only thing we have plenty of. That's why, perhaps, we're no longer the jewel of the Empire. *(Beat)* Want to play fish with me?

REMY: Eat the fish before it eats you? Sure.

(REMY and MEI YEN face each other)

REMY: Fish.

MEI YEN: Next year, my husband may come back from New Haven with an advanced degree. Yale. There's a new democracy movement, perhaps, and he'll be part of it. *(Beat)* Fish.

REMY: When we were climbing the Wall, I had a feeling so high, higher even than making love. *(Beat)* Fish.

MEI YEN: The Emperor had seventy concubines, and still he built the Wall. What do you think? *(Beat)* Fish.

REMY: I'm leaving Sun in Beijing, like a monk without an umbrella. *(Beat)* Fish

MEI YEN: Just a monk. *(Beat)* She didn't need the umbrella after all. She never got to Gansu. *(Beat)* Fish.

REMY: Fish.

MEI YEN: Fish.

(Lights fade.)

(End of scene)

On The Great Wall

(It is almost dark. REMY *and* SUN *walk, as in a dream, completing the circle, ending up where they began, six o'clock, D S center.)*

REMY: Easier going down the Wall than up. There's everyone! We're at the end.

SUN: *And* the beginning.

REMY: If we wanted to climb again. Yes.

SUN: It's almost dark. Another day. I worry about being up here at night with mountain lions and thousand year old rats hidden in the cracks.

REMY: Maybe next year I'll come back. Next summer.

SUN: Next summer will be the Year of the Snake. People born in the Year of the Snake are known for their wisdom and determination. The snake is known for its cleverness. The Year of the Snake is supposed to be more peaceful.

REMY: To the Year of the Snake, then.

SUN: To next year then, the Year of the Snake.

(Lights fade out.)

END OF PLAY

Playwright's note: The next year, June 1989, the Tiananmen Square massacre occurred.

ALMOST IN VEGAS

ALMOST IN VEGAS was written under an N E A grant and opened in New York in May 1985 at The Manhattan Punch Line Theater. The production was first presented by the Pittsburgh Public Theater. The cast and creative contributors were:

ALMA .... April Shawhan
MARGIE .... Susan Cash
LOUIS .... David Little
FELIX .... Mitch McGuire

Director .... Susan Einhorn
Lighting .... Marc Malamud
Sets .... Harry Feiner
Costumes .... Donna Zakowska

CHARACTERS

ALMA LEROY, *thirties, a former classmate of* MARGIE
MARGIE HAMMERSMITH, *thirties, works with* LOUIS *in Hollywood*
FELIX, *bartender*
LOUIS MONACO, *thirties, film executive*

Note: these roles are flexible in age for casting purposes

ACT ONE

Scene One

(Time: Early evening, a little after seven P M. Early December, shortly before Sinatra's death)

(Place: The Birdcage Bar at the Desert Inn in Las Vegas. This is a small bar at the back of the Hotel adjacent to the Casino Cage, the place where all the money is turned in. A Sinatra ballad plays in the background. FELIX, the bartender, stands behind the bar. MARGIE HAMMERSMITH, attractive, slim, sits at the bar having a drink. She is waiting for her lover who is late. We hear the monotonous drone of far away slot machines and the closing and opening of the nearby cage. FELIX sings along to the Sinatra ballad as the lights come up.)

FELIX: We got Sinatra here tonight, you know.

MARGIE: Yes I know.

FELIX: Only one night. So you wouldn't want to miss him.

MARGIE: Lucky I have two tickets.

FELIX: He's getting pudgy I heard.

MARGIE: I hadn't heard.

FELIX: Well that's the word. From God's ear to my mouth.

MARGIE: All I came to hear was "The Voice".

FELIX: Then so far so good. You with the group from Texas? *(Singing)* "The stars at night are big and bright,
BOOM BOOM BOOM BOOM..."

MARGIE: *(Breaking in)* No.

FELIX: *(Singing)* "I left my heart in San Francisco..."

MARGIE: I left my Persian cat in L A.

FELIX: You here by yourself?

MARGIE: I might be.

FELIX: He's late.

MARGIE: *(Holding out her glass)* Another vodka, please.

FELIX: *(Starting to sing)* "Bewitched, bothered and bewildered...I am."
(He pours the vodka and gives it to MARGIE.*)*

MARGIE: For your information, he's coming in from the Coast.

FELIX: Long trip from the Coast if you're coming by camel. *(Continuing to sing "Bewitched")* Sinatra wanted a jacuzzi in his room.

(As he speaks, ALMA LEROY *enters with difficulty, lugging two large suitcases. She is wearing a silk blouse and a skirt. She gets herself settled at the Bar with some difficulty during the following conversation between* FELIX *and* MARGIE. *Once settled, she taps her fingers to the music.)*

FELIX: We don't have jacuzzis. I mean we have them, but not in the rooms. The Sands has them in the rooms, but then they don't do the mints on the pillows.

MARGIE: We were promised the French Suite; they gave us a room in Fantasy Tower. *(Making a face)*

FELIX: Fantasy Tower's top of the line.

MARGIE: Not my line. I had my heart set on something more adult.

FELIX: I could see what I could do. I know the guy on the desk tonight.

MARGIE: I understand the French Suite has birds of paradise painted on the ceiling.

FELIX: The very same ones that sang to Madame DuBarry.

MARGIE: Well that's the room I want.

FELIX: *(Turning to* ALMA*)* Bet you ten bucks you can't sit here all night and not order.

ALMA: What would you count as being all night? *(Staring at* MARGIE *as she continues to talk to* FELIX*)*

FELIX: Hard to say. No night, no day here. They don't like us to display the time openly. That way people don't say "Oh it's time to eat or it's time to sleep". No limits. No perimeters. Keep playing. Fifty blackjack tables, nine hundred slot machines...

ALMA: *(Insistently)* For me to win the bet you said, the ten dollars? What do you mean all night?

FELIX: Quicker ways than that for a lady to make a killing here.

ALMA: You think so?

FELIX: I know so. *(To* MARGIE*)* I know this strip like the backside of my hand. The thing is perseverance. That is the whole thing of this town. *(To* ALMA*)* And chance too. *Serendipity.* Now I am giving you a drink on the house because the house is feeling generous tonight.

ALMA: Make me a Mai Tai and I'll love you forever. *(She is trying to get a better look at* MARGIE.*)*

FELIX: *(To* ALMA*)* You with the group from Texas?

ALMA: God, I hope I don't look like I'm with the group from Texas.

FELIX: *(Pointing to* MARGIE*)* Neither is she. *(Singing)* She's from "Ca-lee-for-nia, here I come..." Aren't you, miss.

MARGIE: *(To* FELIX*)* I beg your pardon.

FELIX: *(Insistently)* Aren't you from California?

MARGIE: The very heart of Hollywood.

ALMA: I'm from Japan. Well not originally. Well it's a long story.

FELIX: I'm sure. So you're having a rendezvous in the desert.

(Giving ALMA *her drink which she drinks too quickly)*

ALMA: I've come to Las Vegas to seek my fortune.

FELIX: Then you must be willing to lose.

ALMA: I have nothing to lose.

FELIX: Average person comes here loses sixty-seven dollars a day. That's average. You don't, however, look average to me.

ALMA: Thank you. I consider that a compliment.

FELIX: No woman I know, however, is average. *(Looking at* MARGIE*)* And I'll warn you that people here are out of their heads, also. Hey, Paradise is just the name of a town in Montana. They don't care here if they put their whole life's savings down the hole. They don't care about nothing except the possibility of winning. Possibility is the American dream, you know.

ALMA: Oh I know. I'm a great believer in anything's possible.

FELIX: *(To* ALMA*)* You got a room with a pool view or a strip view? 'Cause the strip side's noisy. It's worth the extra five bucks to get your quiet poolside, seeing no one uses the pool here. But no one uses anything around here. Best facilities in the world—untouched.

ALMA: I'm a great believer also of using everything to its utmost. That's why God made the earth.

MARGIE: *(To* FELIX*)* Could I interrupt you for an ice cube?

ALMA: *(Still staring at* MARGIE. *There is a silence. She then comes directly over to* MARGIE*)* Excuse me. I don't believe it...Margie? Right? You must think I'm crazy. Is your name Margie? Margie Hammersmith? Margie! It's Alma! Are you Margie?

MARGIE: Margie Hammersmith *(Pause)* Alma?

ALMA: What are you doing in Las Vegas? I don't believe this. God oh God!

MARGIE: Alma LeRoy? Alma?

ALMA: It's me. I bet you don't recognize me. Was I blond yet when you knew me?

MARGIE: I think you had brown hair.

ALMA: Yeah, well that was my regular hair. Hey, you look terrific! Oh God!

(She gives MARGIE *an enormous hug which* MARGIE *reluctantly responds to.)*

MARGIE: What are you doing in Las Vegas?

ALMA: I thought everyone should see it once before they die.

FELIX: *(Handing* MARGIE *her drink)* Ice, Margie. Another Mai Tai, Alma?

ALMA: *(Pausing, then)* Yeah. Sure. On the house. Right?

FELIX: *(Pouring it)* The house is feeling extra-generous tonight. Old Blue Eyes is expected to rake in the biggest casino take in history.

MARGIE: I'll take care of it, Alma. This is an occasion. Me. You. Sinatra. *(To* FELIX*)* On my tab, please.

ALMA: *(To* FELIX*)* We were in the same class in high school.

MARGIE: The guy I'm meeting here is running late. He's coming in from the Coast.

FELIX: And ten to one she's mad.

MARGIE: *(Shaking her head)* Not yet.

*(*FELIX *hands the drink to* ALMA*.)*

ALMA: Well I was on my way back from Tokyo, Japan. I've been there ten years. I stopped off to see my sister in San Francisco and then here I am. Hey, I didn't go to our high school reunion last year. Did you?

MARGIE: I didn't know we had one.

ALMA: Well I didn't go either, but if I did I would have gotten the prize for coming the longest—all the way from Tokyo. God, I don't believe this. You look terrific. Are you married?

MARGIE: Nope.

ALMA: God, nobody's married anymore. Nobody wants connections. *(To* FELIX*)* Are you married?

FELIX: Do I look stupid? Put myself in a dying institution?

ALMA: I've got two kids, a girl and a boy, Judy and Jimmy. They're back in Tokyo with their nurse. Everyone in Tokyo has a nurse. I'm on a trial separation from my husband. He's a Captain in the Army. Hey, what are you doing in California, Margie?

FELIX: She's a movie star.

MARGIE: *(To* ALMA*)* I'm with M G M.

FELIX:	ALMA:
Jackpot!	Dynamite!

FELIX: *(Singing)* "Bewitched, bothered and bewildered...I am."
Hey, can you get me into the movies?

MARGIE: Sales and distribution.

ALMA: You did it!

MARGIE: Did *what*?

ALMA: Well what does that mean exactly, sales and distribution?

MARGIE: To market, to market, what sells best where. For example, you *can't*
send the Rolling Stones to Kansas, but you can send Frank Sinatra anywhere.

ALMA: Oh he's popular in Tokyo too.

MARGIE: He sings what people want to hear.

FELIX: *(Singing, simulating Sinatra)* "Saturday night is the loneliest night of
the week. It's when my baby..." *(Speaking the rest, as he really doesn't know the
song exactly—just the gist)* "...does something or other."

MARGIE: *(Whispering playfully)* Sometimes, on Sundays, I listen to Sinatra in
place of going to church.

ALMA: Margie sold the most ads for the school play. The dress I made for
her part.... *(To* MARGIE*)* Remember, *(Back to* FELIX*)* it was pale blue taffeta
and with little pearls I sewed on...I was in costumes...in the shape of daisies.
We used fake yellow jewels for the center.

MARGIE: It was a musical and I couldn't sing.

ALMA: Well the picture's in the yearbook. Margie was really gorgeous.
A born star.

FELIX: I bet.

ALMA: *(To* MARGIE*)* Hey, are you a Pisces?

MARGIE: March fifteenth.

ALMA: I knew you were a Pisces. They're over achievers. I'm a Sagittarius.
I wish I wasn't. *(To* FELIX*)* You know, she was one of the most popular girls
in the class. *(To* MARGIE*)* I can't believe you're not married.

MARGIE: I must be very particular.

ALMA: She had every boy in school *going* and *coming.*

MARGIE: *(To* ALMA*)* Spare me, don't dredge up all that old stuff.

(Pause)

ALMA: *(To* MARGIE*)* Where are you staying?

MARGIE: Here in the hotel... *(Directed to* FELIX*)* In some rooms we're hoping to change.

ALMA: Poolside or stripside because the pool side's more peaceful, but I don't mind the noise. In fact I welcome it. Noise is life. I'm here alone but I guess you're not. *(Pause)* I thought bartenders were supposed to listen.

FELIX: *(Testily)* If the lady desires, I'd like to ring up the desk and give them some Glory Hallelujah regarding *not delivering on a promise.* Only thing is, if the French Suite's taken, is to move down to the Gothic suite, which was vacated I understand, in a hurry, early this morning.

MARGIE: You're a sweetheart; and could you tell me where the nearest public phone is? *(To* ALMA*)* I'll be right back, Alma.

FELIX: Margie's getting antsy. I can see she's not a lady to be kept in waiting. *(To* MARGIE*)* Down by the Casino Cage, next to the fountain with the urinating angel.

MARGIE: Thanks. *(She starts to exit.)*

ALMA: You need a quarter? *(Digging in her purse)* I think I've got one. God don't you hate bars? They're so impersonal. *(She continues to dig in her purse.)*

MARGIE: Thanks but I have it.

*(*MARGIE *exits.* ALMA *continues to dig in her purse not noticing* MARGIE*'s exit.)*

ALMA: I spend half my life in a phone booth. I'm in one place, I'm always making plans to be in the next. My husband, the Captain, says I'm always "between engagements". *(Putting down her purse, looking up and seeing that* MARGIE*'s gone)* Isn't she a knockout? *(To* FELIX*)* I would have given anything to be like her.

FELIX: Drafty.

ALMA: Oh no. Mysterious. I am such an open book. I wish I wasn't. We were kind of real good friends. Well she was pretty smart. And she was also pretty. So she was pretty busy. But one thing about me—no matter—I'm loyal. *(Digging in her purse again)* If I give you fifty cents would you play something for me on the jukebox, something American, but soft, like Barry Manilow or Barbara Streisand? I don't know what's good anymore. I've been away so long.

FELIX: It's up to one dollar.

ALMA: *(Digging in her purse)* Eighteen years since I saw Margie Hammersmith and then I go and meet her in Las Vegas, U S of A.

FELIX: Frank Sinatra on the house. *(Turning on the jukebox)* Let me call them, see if I can influence this switch. You scratch my back around here, I'll scratch yours. *(Going to use the house phone)* And I got even money on it's going to be a brew-ha-ha of a night.

(FELIX *exits. Frank Sinatra's music comes up. "Strangers in the Night". ALMA starts to dance with herself. LOUIS MONACO enters carrying a suit bag. He looks around the bar, watches ALMA dance. He waits...then....)*

LOUIS: Excuse me...excuse me, Miss...Miss... You've haven't seen a woman waiting here, have you?

(ALMA *shakes her head "no" and continues dancing, humming to herself. LOUIS speaks louder.)*

LOUIS: Dark-haired? Slim?

(ALMA *shrugs, continues to dance.)*

ALMA: I haven't been looking.

LOUIS: She left a message at the desk, said "See you in the Birdcage Bar". Is there another Birdcage Bar?

ALMA: *(Still dancing)* Could be. It's a very gigantic hotel.

LOUIS: *(Reading the note MARGIE left him)* "The little Birdcage Bar down by the Casino Cage where they turn in the chips." The rest is personal.

(Pause)

ALMA: *(Nodding towards O S)* There's your cage. *(Nodding to the bar)* Here's your bar.

LOUIS: Because I'm very late.

ALMA: Timing's everything.

LOUIS: You bet. *(Pause)* Well did anyone leave a message here?

ALMA: *(Stopping her dancing, looking on top of the bar and under it)* Let me look... Nope... No messages here. Just ice.

LOUIS: That's funny. *(Sitting down at a bar stool)* She's supposed to be here.

ALMA: I wouldn't know. I'm not my sister's keeper.

LOUIS: Witty.

(ALMA *continues to dance.)*

LOUIS: The bartender doesn't come soon, I'm going to help myself.

ALMA: Go ahead. I wouldn't squeal.

(LOUIS *goes behind the bar, pours himself a drink, and swallows it down quickly. ALMA continues to dance. LOUIS continues to look around the bar.)*

LOUIS: Could I ask you to keep an eye out while I check out the hotel. She has brown hair. A dozen guys probably tried to pick her up by now. She's a knockout.

ALMA: I couldn't promise. *(Continuing to dance)* I just came in from Tokyo and I'm trying to get rid of my jet lag.

LOUIS: *(Getting up, starting to leave, then sarcastically)* Thanks a lot. Have yourself a wonderful evening, Miss.

ALMA: Wait a minute! There was a woman here before, skinny, with dark hair. She works for M G M.

LOUIS: *(Coming back excitedly)* That's her! That's Margie!

ALMA: I believe she left for the airport.

LOUIS: That couldn't be. I just came from the airport.

ALMA: Isn't that life? Paths cross at the wrong time. She was very angry. I heard her distinctively say "airport".

LOUIS: How long ago was she here?

ALMA: I wasn't especially counting.

LOUIS: When did she leave?

ALMA: You just missed her. If this was the same person.

LOUIS: *(Taking out a flight schedule)* Next flight to L A's at ten P M. *(He checks his watch.)*

ALMA: *If* she's going to L A.

LOUIS: Did she tell you where she was going?

ALMA: She wasn't the kind of person that tells you that stuff.

LOUIS: Sounds like Margie. Could I ask you a favor? If she comes back, would you tell her Louis Monaco was here and for her to stay put in the bar and wait? I'm going to take a look around.

ALMA: Sure. I'll tell her if I see her. I wouldn't want to lose her if I were you. You should try the airport. That's what this woman said.

(FELIX enters during this speech, remaining in the shadows.)

LOUIS: It's not like I didn't warn her I could get tied up.

ALMA: Well she's not here. I distinctly heard her say "Airport".

LOUIS: Jesus, this is ridiculous. She's probably in one of her snits. *(He starts to leave.)*

ALMA: *(Calling after him)* Hey, I hope you don't have trouble getting a cab. I had to wait half an hour at the bus station. Everything's tied up because of Sinatra being in town.

LOUIS: I'll find one thanks. *(He exits.)*

ALMA: *(To herself)* You're welcome. I'm sure you will.

FELIX: *(Entering the lit part of the Stage. He pauses. ALMA smiles tentatively.)* I thought you said you were loyal.

ALMA: He just wants one thing from her.

FELIX: Why don't you allow her the pleasure of his attempt.

ALMA: 'Cause I'm a better friend, or could be.

FELIX: You want more than that one thing.

ALMA: Oh I want more things than the world's even thought up yet.

FELIX: Bet your bottom dollar he'll be right back.

ALMA: It depends how bad he wants whatever it is he wants.

(MARGIE *enters.*)

MARGIE: I couldn't get through. They kept me on hold. I'll call from my room.

FELIX: Which could be changing any hour if luck's on our side. People in the French don't want the Gothic but are considering a move to the more expensive Flamingo Suite if we give it for the same price.

MARGIE: *(To* FELIX*)* I shouldn't unpack then?

FELIX: Up to you.

ALMA: *(To* MARGIE*)* You're going upstairs?

MARGIE: It's been a zoo of a week. I'm exhausted.

ALMA: Oh, me too. *Ex*-hausted.

MARGIE: I want to iron a dress, change the time on our dinner reservation.

FELIX: I'll do it.

MARGIE: *I'll* do it. *(To* ALMA*)* But if you ever get out to the Coast, Alma, I'd love to meet for lunch. *(Taking her card out, handing it to* ALMA*)* Here's my card. Maybe I could show you around. Get you a tour of the studio.

ALMA: *(Taking it disappointedly)* That sounds like fun. *(Pause, still holding the card, reading it)* But I was wondering if I could use your room, Margie. Just for a minute. It sounds silly but I don't trust public facilities. Do you know that in Japan all the public restrooms are spotless to beautiful, little flower arrangements on all the washbasins.

MARGIE: I was planning a nap. If we really got gabbing, what all, we'd be off....

ALMA: Well when do you want to get together then? Almost eighteen years! I mean we haven't even started to scratch the surface. Geez, I bet it would take us a week to catch up! A lot of water under the dam since West St Louis High. Just the whole Pacific Ocean.

MARGIE: How long will you be in town?

ALMA: Overnight, probably.

MARGIE: Let me take your hotel number. *(Taking some matches off the bar)* Here. Write it on the back of the matchbook. *(She holds out the matchbook.)*

ALMA: The town's booked up solid because of Sinatra. There's not a room around. *(Pause)* All I want to do is use your toilet. *(Whispering loudly)* I have my period and I'm flowing like the Red Sea. *(Pause)* I wouldn't intrude.

MARGIE: Alma, we've been planing this weekend for months. We have some intimate things we want to talk about. I'm not being unkind, just honest.

ALMA: You mean you think he's going to ask you to marry him.

MARGIE: That's not what I mean.

ALMA: You gonna ask him?

MARGIE: Something like that.

ALMA: You want to screw. You can say it.

MARGIE: No!

FELIX: Will you two have anything else? Name your desire.

ALMA: *(Whispering loudly to* MARGIE*)* Oh God! I think I'm coming through!

MARGIE: Are you sure?

ALMA: I couldn't be surer. Oh God!

MARGIE: *(To* ALMA, *reluctantly, then impatiently, and angrily, as if to a whining child)* Okay! Okay! *(To* FELIX*)* If someone's looking for me I'm in my room. *(To* ALMA*)* Well come on, Alma. Move it.

ALMA: You really want me to?

*(*ALMA *struggles with all her luggage which* MARGIE *sees for the first time.)*

MARGIE: *You* asked *me.* Just do what you have to do.

ALMA: And we'll go from there.

MARGIE: And *you'll* go from there.

FELIX: Ladies... the bill.

*(*FELIX *holds up the bill.)*

MARGIE: Charge, please, the Tower, Room 1222. *(She signs the bill.)*

FELIX: Triple Deuce. Got it.

MARGIE: For the moment—courtesy of M G M.

(The women exit, ALMA *dragging her luggage.)*

(End of scene)

Scene Two

(Time: Fifteen minutes later)

(Place: The Fantasy Tower. It is opulently furnished, but in good taste, high windows, lots of glass and chrome, perhaps mirrors on the ceiling or on the walls. There is a sunken living room. Set allowing there could be a spiral staircase up to the bedroom level. It is possible, also, to stage the play simply, in two spaces. MARGIE presses a dress with a small traveling iron. Sound of a toilet flushing. ALMA calls from the bathroom.)

ALMA: *(O S)* Did you catch the bathroom? *(Talking as she enters)* It's all pink and white marble. You can see the desert out the window if you stand on your tiptoes on the tub. So I said to him, "Malcolm",—that's what I call my husband—"the marriage is a farce. We hate each other." I didn't tell him why I hated him, but I know why he hated me. He's a very quiet person.

MARGIE: *(Distractedly)* How come you married him then?

ALMA: Oh, 'cause I was in love with him. Of course life didn't turn out exactly like I expected. I'm a very familied person. What am I supposed to do now? Go to singles bars? *(Beat)* You want to know what he looked like? He was a real hunk. He was a semi-famous football player for the University of Indiana. He's tall and he has whitish hair which used to be blond, and blue eyes and a nice mouth, not too big or little, and a hairy chest, if you like that. I like that.

MARGIE: *(Distractedly)* Mmmm.

ALMA: Though once I made love with a man who was as smooth as a billiard ball and I found that surprisingly sexy.

MARGIE: I could see that, the feel of that.

ALMA: He was a wrestler. He didn't have a hair on his chest. All smooth.

MARGIE: I could see where smooth would be interesting.

ALMA: But that's it. In given circumstances, you don't know. You can't predict life like a dot. You might meet someone bald and you like the inside, so then you like the outside, or vice-versa.

MARGIE: Could be.

ALMA: Oh anything can be. That's what sex is really about. That children come from it is what I don't understand. It's supposed to be the most beautiful thing on earth, but sometimes I think it's the saddest. That's why you have to do it in two's. It's too sad to do alone. *(Pause)* I sent you a postcard from Hawaii on the way over. It had a picture of a palm tree on it.

MARGIE: I'm sorry. I don't remember.

ALMA: Well I sent it. It had a picture of a palm tree and a pineapple.

MARGIE: Then thank you. *(Pause)* All set?

ALMA: Under control.

MARGIE: Glad I could help.

(Pause. They look at each other.)

ALMA: And I met Jerry Foster.

MARGIE: Jerry Foster! Where'd you see Jerry Foster?

ALMA: Tokyo. He was over on business. He's in ball bearings. He said you two wrote while you were in college.

MARGIE: Jerry Foster. That was sure the other side of the road. One New Year's Eve he came up to school. I didn't go home that year. I had my own apartment. He decided to read *all* of *The Fountainhead* aloud to me. *(Pause)* We got to Chapter Three...

ALMA: I told him we wrote too because I was embarrassed to say we didn't. *(Pause)* Tokyo was very boring. All I did was play bridge and I wasn't very good at it either. The other officers' wives said I talked too much. "Either play or leave", they said. Well I was leaving anyway. *(Pause)* Malcolm said I was too sexual for my own good.

MARGIE: He was probably frightened of you.

ALMA: I don't think so. He wasn't scared of the Colonel's daughter and I didn't think she was that pretty. *(Pause, picking up the room service menu)*

MARGIE: *(Finishing pressing the dress)* Jerry wanted to get married, move back to St Louis, in the days when tradition was getting very untraditional.

ALMA: He has a factory in New Orleans and one in Atlanta.

MARGIE: *(Cutting her off)* I don't want to hear it. Finis. *(Silence)* Is he single?

(ALMA shakes her head "no".)

ALMA: *(Still reading the room service menu)* The turkey club sounds good...don't you love to read Room Service stuff..."chunks of turkey, wedges of tomato". Actually, I'm famished. They used to serve beautiful meals on airplanes, but these were just little sandwiches.

MARGIE: I'm supposed to go out for dinner, Alma.

ALMA: You still going?

MARGIE: I don't know.

ALMA: Well when are you going to know? Because we could eat together.

MARGIE: I don't know when I'm going to know.

ALMA: No...of course you don't.... *(Pause)* Do you mind if I order the club?

MARGIE: If he comes we're going to leave... or stay... when he comes.

ALMA: That's okay. *(Still reading the menu)* Okay? *(Picking up the phone)* Okay if I order a drink? It's number three for room service.

MARGIE: No it isn't.

ALMA: I'm really hungry.

MARGIE: So am I.

(ALMA puts the phone down. Pause)

ALMA: I read an article in a magazine a couple of years ago. *REAL LIFE SUCCESSES.* You were in a white suit.

MARGIE: That awful picture!

ALMA: What I didn't think was so good was they told your salary.

MARGIE: Oh it's gone way up since then. That was the beginning of a real roll for me. I started out there, this green Beauty Queen, two years of acting lessons under my belt, doing commercials. I had a detergent and an antacid my first year. Pretty good! Second year, I got a small part in a horror film, about a forest fire that spreads over the *entire* country. The director was connected up the wazoo at M G M, and one thing led to another, and there I was with my own office. And on top of that, I met Louis—that's the guy who's coming here. He's in global distribution, and I'm regional. He kept encouraging me—"You're doing it! You're doing it!"...pumping me up, you know. Then they did the article and everything took off. *(Making a signal with her hand outstretched like an airplane taking off)* Here I am with my own investment portfolio and a real Burburry raincoat... *(Explaining in case ALMA doesn't understand)* The plaid ones with the lining. If you buy them in London it's cheaper. That's what I did.

ALMA: I'm planning on getting a job in St Louis. I can type.

MARGIE: Good.

(Pause)

ALMA: Hey, want to go down and see Sinatra if your date doesn't show?

MARGIE: It's highly unlikely he won't show.

ALMA: Oh showing up's three quarters of life I think.

MARGIE: We have tickets. Louis will get here. Louis loves Sinatra. *(Pause)* Alma, are you leaving or not?

ALMA: Well he isn't here yet.

MARGIE: *(Pause)* Five minutes. That's it.

ALMA: That's what my sister said too. *(Hiccoughing, continuing to hiccough throughout the rest of the scene randomly until indicated to stop)* When I got off the plane in San Francisco, I called her right away from the airport. She lives on one of those curlicue streets by the bay, straight across from Alcatraz, and I said "Boy, do I ever need a sister", and she said "Okay, I got five minutes..."

MARGIE: That's not nice.

ALMA: That's my sister. *(Hiccoughing)* Sorry. Excuse me. Well I'm certainly not going to kill myself over it, so I hopped right over to the bus station. I've got to watch my pennies now that I'm on my own.

MARGIE: Fuck her. *(Pause)* Louis' plane's probably late.

ALMA: Probably. People are saying the traffic's perscrewey because of Sinatra.... *(Hiccoughing)* Excuse me. I always hiccough when I'm nervous. Why don't you call the airport?

MARGIE: He'll come when he comes.

ALMA: Unless he doesn't, and hey, if that happens.... *(Hiccoughing)* Just don't pay attention to them. And this person you're involved with who is coming here tonight doesn't come tonight, it's not the end of the world because the only thing that's the end of the world is the end of the world. And hey, if that happens would you mind sharing the room seeing the town's booked up 'cause of you know who?

MARGIE: You don't have a room?

ALMA: I could use the couch. And I'd pitch in. Thank God money's no object. I know some women split they leave with nothing. Not me. I emptied out all the bank accounts. I'm very good at getting first in line. *(Hiccoughing)*

MARGIE: If I say yes, he could still come.

ALMA: Well the world is full of possibilities but it's always better to know. And everything with a beginning has an end, which is a good thing regarding bad things, which gives you hope about things like hiccoughs and natural things like the flood in the Bible.

MARGIE: Alma... *(Pause)* You're driving me out of my mind.

ALMA: I know. This is silly. *(Hiccoughing)* I'm sorry.

(MARGIE *goes to the phone.*)

ALMA: What are you doing?

MARGIE: *(Dialing, then speaking)* American Airlines? Flight 447 from L A to Las Vegas due in about six... Thank you. *(She slams down the phone.)* It landed a few hours ago.

ALMA: *(Hiccoughing)* You know, I know one woman who's been divorced four years and she's never gone out on a date. *(Hiccoughing)* That's scary. *(Hiccoughing)* Sorry.

MARGIE: Will you stop apologizing!

ALMA: Sorry... *(Realizing she's apologized again, Pause)* You make me nervous.

MARGIE: If you don't like it, leave!

ALMA: No, I like it. You say, "fuck everyone".

MARGIE: *(Sarcastically)* Oh sure. That's me. The streets are literally lined with bodies I've trampled... Shit! You know all the planning that's gone into this weekend? If something happened he would have called. Oh God, I will die if something happened. I've been treading so gently, like a Geisha girl, up and down his back, checking every detail, everything perfect... time, clothes, room, mood... Alma, I came out west planning for quicksilver, smashed my way out of St. Louis... "Don't be sentimental. Run for your life!" Not "Go marry Jerry Foster, have a family, buy a house, and go to the Caribbean for your twenty-fifth anniversary..." *(Pause)* Listen, you can use the couch if he doesn't get here. Shit!

ALMA: Gee, that's wonderful. Thank you! *(Pause)* And anyway, you have your job.

MARGIE: *(Pause)* Anyway, *you* have your kids.

ALMA: They're sure a responsibility, like a pin in your heart.

MARGIE: At least they're something in your heart.

ALMA: One of mine's dyslexic...the boy. He has trouble with his reading. *(Pause)* Margie, I haven't had a bite since the little things they served on the plane.

MARGIE: Go order what you want.

ALMA: *(Picking up the phone without hesitation)* Room 1222. Fantasy Tower. The turkey deluxe. *(Aside to MARGIE)* It comes with french fries.

MARGIE: M G M's paying. The sky's the limit.

ALMA: *(Back into the phone)* And one large O J, fresh. *(Hanging up)* They didn't have oranges in Japan, or they did, but they were too expensive, Malcolm said. They had to get them from California. They said it could be a wait on the turkey club. Service is all backed up 'cause of Sinatra. Sure you don't want anything?

MARGIE: I can't eat when I'm upset.

ALMA: *(Continuing though MARGIE's next speech)* It's okay because I don't mind eating alone. On nights Malcolm wasn't home, the maid would feed the kids early. Everyone in Tokyo has a maid.

MARGIE: *(Overlapping ALMA's speech)* I'm calling his secretary at home. *(Getting her address book out)*

ALMA: *(Continuing through MARGIE's next speech)* Then she'd set the table with flowers and candles and all, and I'd sit there and she'd serve me, all by myself, many courses, and every one of them would have a name.

MARGIE: *(Overlapping with* ALMA*)* No I'm not! *(Closing book)* I'm not calling.

ALMA: Oh they do everything beautiful in Tokyo. I would have liked to read a magazine or paper, but I think that would have looked rude.

MARGIE: I am getting very depressed, Alma. Could you do me a favor and shut up!

ALMA: *(Nodding "yes" tentatively, then rolling right along)* What you have to do is make your way up and over it. Malcolm called me "sunshine". Even when he saw me off at the airport. He gave me a peck and said "See you sunshine", though he was just saying it and I turned around because I was crying and I didn't want the children to see. My boy Jimmy has dyslexia. It means he reads backwards.... I said that.... When I get enough money, I'm going to send for them. Hey, I think my hiccoughs stopped.

(The phone rings. MARGIE goes to answer.)

MARGIE: *(Relieved, into the phone)* Hello... Louis... Where are you?

ALMA: *(While MARGIE is on the phone, speaking over MARGIE)* Yup. I picked myself right up and took myself over to Las Vegas before going home for good. My mother died while I was in Tokyo. I didn't come back for the funeral because my sister said there was no sense, but I'm going to visit her grave and maybe plant lilacs around it.

MARGIE: *(Flirtatiously into the phone)* No I wasn't there because I was here...waiting. No, I know where I was. I'm not angry. Just come... Goodbye... Hurry... *(Hanging up)*

ALMA: He's on his way.

MARGIE: I'm sorry. Do you think we could get together tomorrow?

ALMA: I never got my turkey club.

MARGIE: The Dining Room's still open. Everyplace here stays open all night. It's unreal.

ALMA: Maybe I could wait until Room Service comes and take it with me—where we ordered it.

MARGIE: He's coming right over. *(Pause)* I wish you'd leave, Alma. Please. It's not like I didn't tell you.

ALMA: You could have told him not to come. He was so late anyways. I don't know why you'd want him. He sounds like a loser to me.

MARGIE: He's very attractive. He's nice to me. *(Pause)* He turns me on. *(Pause)* I don't have to explain. This is embarrassing.

ALMA: Men have always been nice to you. All you have to do is wiggle your finger. I'll just use the toilet again before I go. I always have to use the toilet a lot when I'm nervous. *(She exits. From bathroom)* You know when I first saw you downstairs I was going to make believe I didn't see you because you always intimidated me. I think you were stuck-up.

MARGIE: *(Calling back through the door)* I'm an extremely private person.

ALMA: You had every color cashmere sweater under the sun.

MARGIE: My aunt was a buyer for Neiman-Marcus.

ALMA: I thought you were rich.

MARGIE: *(Toilet flushes)* No. My aunt was a buyer.

ALMA: *(As she re-enters)* Is he married?

MARGIE: They don't sleep together.

ALMA: Because if he is, he'll never leave her, if that's what you're thinking.

MARGIE: You have no idea what I'm thinking.

ALMA: *(Intimidated by MARGIE's assertive evasiveness)* 'Cause who knows the future and there's certainly nothing you can do about the past.

MARGIE: That's correct.

ALMA: *(Getting her things together)* Hey, if it doesn't work out, I'll be downstairs in the Bar. Now everything's changed, you know. Now everyone knows we women have to stick together.

MARGIE: I'm sorry, but I've been counting on this weekend.

ALMA: Well, the best laid plans... Listen, maybe it's my lucky night. I could hit it big in the Casino. One quarter and zingo!

(Pause)

MARGIE: Alma...I think you've turned out very nicely.

ALMA: You do?

MARGIE: And I'm sorry you're having trouble.

ALMA: Thank you.

(A knock at the door)

MARGIE: Louis. It's probably Louis. *(Calling)* Coming!

ALMA: *(Hurriedly)* I don't want to meet him.

MARGIE: *(Pointing to the bedroom area of the suite)* Use the other door then.

(ALMA starts to exit.)

MARGIE: Hey, you left your bags! *(Calling after her)*

ALMA: *(Calling from the other room)* I'll get them later!

MARGIE: *(Grabbing ALMA's bags, going after ALMA)* Take your bags, Alma!

ALMA: *(O S)* I'll get them later!

(Another knock at the door)

MARGIE: Coming!

(MARGIE flings open the door and FELIX enters. He pulls in the silver serving cart, shuts the door quickly, and pushes the cart into the room. Pointing to the cart, playfully)

MARGIE: You! I thought it was someone else.

FELIX: Room Service! What's your desire?

MARGIE: *(Pointing)* By the window. *(Reminding him)* About the room change.

FELIX: I got news!

MARGIE: *(Excited)* We've got the other room.

FELIX: Not exactly. Couple in the French don't care for the Flamingo, *even* at the same price; don't like all that pink. So, I suggested an exact switch, but they want to know if this room is so *fan*-tastic, how come you want out?

MARGIE: Tell them I'm more grounded in reality.

FELIX: *(Looking around)* I see he's not here yet.

MARGIE: He is *in transit*, thank you.

FELIX: It's Sinatra. He's fouling up everything.

MARGIE: It's probably Sinatra. Yes.

FELIX: Where'd your friend Alma go?

MARGIE: She had to leave.

FELIX: A pity.

MARGIE: Yes it is.

(FELIX takes a french fry off the plate.)

MARGIE: I'll sign for it so you can get back downstairs. I imagine it's busy.

FELIX: Busiest place outside the Courthouse. *(Looking out the window, spotting Sinatra down below)* HEY! There he is! There's Sinatra! You want to believe it! He looks terrible. Face is all puffy. Doesn't look too good for Francis Albert.

MARGIE: Maybe he'll die here. He could lie in state in the Flamingo Suite.

FELIX: *(Singing)* "Strangers in the night..."

MARGIE: And be enshrined at the Hollywood Bowl.

FELIX: *(Continuing to sing)* Strangers in the night, Exchanging glances, Love may come and go, And take its chances, Du bee du bee du bee, Du bee du bee da... You know you can't sing like that unless you've been belly to belly with reality. *(Pause)* Bet you twenty blind he's standing you up.

MARGIE: I think you're a trouble maker.

FELIX: I still think he's a no-show.

MARGIE: Thank you and you can put the tray directly by the window.

FELIX: I see it every day—women up in rooms, waiting. Bad for the heart.

MARGIE: He's a top executive with M G M with a complicated schedule.

FELIX: Five billion people in the world. Think of all the possible combinations, infinite as stars in the sky. So you wouldn't want to settle.

MARGIE: *(Getting a pencil from her purse and picking up the bill and signing it)* Signed. All set. There you are.

FELIX: And here *you* are. And that's the new age. Stand alone. So when the cheese stands alone, *what?* He's lonely. You know, I've got this friend, he's got this house down in Martha's Vineyard, and Jimmy Cagney used to live across the water. It's true. He even got me his autograph for my collection. I've got Ethel Merman..."To Felix with kisses...", Marilyn Monroe...that's all she wrote was her name..."Marilyn..."

MARGIE: I'm sure it's very valuable.

FELIX: Oh yeah. I get offers on my autographs, but nothing doing. Well, Cagney had this boat with three sails and a big American flag. It was called the "Margie".

MARGIE: Oh I'm sure.

FELIX: No it's true. They say his hair was all white at the end and he had a beard. Can't hold back the doors of time. You ever seen Tony Bennett?

MARGIE: No I never saw Tony Bennett! I never saw James Cagney!

FELIX: *(Cutting her off)* What I think is Cagney probably had a girlfriend named Margie. Unless he was in love with some actress who played Margie in the movies. *(Singing)* "Margie, I'm always dreaming of you, Margie, I'd give the world to see you..."

(Coming closer to MARGIE *as she pulls away)*

FELIX: "Oh oh oh oh oh oh oh oh, Da da da da..."

MARGIE: *(Breaking into his song)* If you don't leave I'm calling management.

FELIX: I'm just passing the time of *(Singing)* "Night and Day...you are the one..."

MARGIE: I'm paying for this room.

FELIX: Who are you kidding? *He's* paying for this room. And if he doesn't show, no one's paying for the room.

MARGIE: I have my own credit cards. *(Pause)* And if you try something, I'll call the desk. You won't succeed in seducing me.

FELIX: Hope springs eternal in the human breast. And we only accept major cards—Master, Visa, American Express.

MARGIE: *(Flipping through her credit cards, finding the ones he's mentioned)* Got it! Got it! Got it! My friend's going to be here in a minute, so you'd better scram.

FELIX: Why don't you scram, which you would if you were smart, instead of hanging around a crazy place like this. Go find your friend, I mean Alma, who's sitting in the bar because I don't think she has anyplace else to go. *(Pause)* I was considering making a play for you, Margie, but I lost interest. Can't find anything to put my hands on. And better not eat the turkey. It's not fresh. Flash frozen.

MARGIE: It's not for me.

FELIX: Then especially don't eat it. *(He exits humming "Margie".)*

(End of scene)

Scene Three

(Time: A half hour later, Nine P M)

(Place: Hotel room. MARGIE is getting dressed.)

(LOUIS enters, with luggage.)

MARGIE: Finally...you're here!

LOUIS: Wild horses couldn't keep me away, *(Throwing down his suitbag)* but some screwball almost did. *(Embracing her)* Oh good. Oh good.

MARGIE: God, am I glad to see you! *(Kissing him)* You're very late for dinner, Mr Monaco.

LOUIS: *(Kissing her)* Is that so? Then how about dessert?

MARGIE: *(Grabbing his ass)* How about a hot cross bun?

LOUIS: *(Grabbing her ass)* How about it?

MARGIE: Oh God, I love your ass!

LOUIS: *(Kissing her, never missing a beat)* It *is* a great ass, isn't it?

MARGIE: It has, let's say, topography.

LOUIS: Not to be ignored... *(Touching MARGIE's breasts)* Beautiful breasts. Jesus, breasts like honey.

MARGIE: Both of them?

LOUIS: *(Continuing to caress her)* Without discrimination, yes. *(Burying his head in her breasts)* I could live inside those breasts, hide from the world in these, get smothered, and probably die a happy death. I've been trailing your scent all over town... *(Kissing her again)* I had to wait twenty minutes for a cab from the airport.

MARGIE: It's Sinatra.

LOUIS: I know. He's the hottest number in Vegas.

MARGIE: Maybe not.

LOUIS: Oh?

MARGIE: Oh. How do you like the room?

LOUIS: *(Not even looking)* Super.

MARGIE: Because they gave the one we wanted, with the lucite bathtub, to someone else.

LOUIS: *(Still embracing her)* We'll have to make do then, with our own entertainment. Let's just barricade the door and never go back to real life.

MARGIE: Lunatic city out there. This flake from my old high school is in the hotel. All the crazies must land here.

LOUIS: No kidding. I got to the desk, you weren't in the room, and no one could give me a straight answer. And I couldn't find you, so I figured you were mad because I was late.

MARGIE: And I thought you changed your mind.

LOUIS: I don't change my mind once I decide. But I figured you were in a snit, and if I could find you, I'd get you out of it.

MARGIE: We won't say how.

LOUIS: A good tickle.

MARGIE: *That* cheap.

LOUIS: But someone now gives me a cockamamie story, so I go back to the airport, like a dope, because you're not *here*, only you're not *there*.

MARGIE: And all the time I'm lying in wait.

LOUIS: Oh the pressure with women like you who are insatiable! My neck's all tensed up. It's doing that tense thing again. *(He moves his head doing neck exercises.)*

MARGIE: You want me to rub it for you?

LOUIS: All I need is your very skilled fingers.

MARGIE: Anywhere... Come here.

(He does. She unbuttons his shirt and starts to massage.)

LOUIS: Your turn will come and the last shall be first.

MARGIE: I moved up our dinner reservations. The show's at eleven.

LOUIS: Good plan...towards the left.

MARGIE: *(Massaging)* Move towards the left.

LOUIS: We'll eat first.

MARGIE: The Riviera Room.

LOUIS: The Riviera Room... oysters.

MARGIE: Oysters. *(Still massaging)*

LOUIS: On the half shell.

MARGIE: Do you really like the room? It has a front view and the desert's out the back, but you have to stand on the bathtub to see it.

LOUIS: I don't give a damn about the room. We could be in East Cincinnati. *(Caressing her, touching her dress)* But, I like you in this.

MARGIE: You know me. I like everything pretty.

LOUIS: *(Pause)* I have to tell you, Margie. This is the first time in months I've been away with no junk intruding, no reality. I feel like floating. *(Pause)* Remember the St Francis Hotel? The four-poster bed?

MARGIE: Slip right down...

LOUIS: Into the show. Ouch! Gentler. You're squeezing.

MARGIE: Sorry.

LOUIS: Better.

MARGIE: Good.

LOUIS: I think you're getting it.

MARGIE: I've been getting it for a long time.

LOUIS: *(As MARGIE massages)* So I've noticed...oh...good...right there... oh yeah...yeah. *(Continuing his story)* Then we'll come back upstairs....

MARGIE: They have satin sheets.

LOUIS: They do?

MARGIE: I checked. *(Beat)* I was worried something happened, and after I got a cat sitter for the weekend in addition to a matching bra and bikini, peach colored.

LOUIS: If it works, then it works.

MARGIE: Oh shut up. It always works.

LOUIS: And what about the conference in London last year?

MARGIE: Aha. You think about me.

LOUIS: We should go back. We didn't get to see half the sights. Didn't even see the Tower of London.

MARGIE: But this is the first time it's not business.

(Pause)

LOUIS: At the board meeting this morning, which was very boring, I fantasized about how we'd come in the door and I'd pull off your clothes. We wouldn't even make it to the bed—on the floor...we'd make love like crazy people, wild, like animals. Then I'd turn off all the lights and we'd fall asleep—right on the carpet.

MARGIE: Before or after Sinatra?

LOUIS: Right in the middle. We'd have to leave. I just told you. We're like wild animals.

MARGIE: Sometimes I think what if we'd met way back; then, everything would be different.

LOUIS: We'd be old and married and bored. *(He starts unpacking.)*

MARGIE: Maybe.

LOUIS: This is better.

MARGIE: How?

LOUIS: It's more interesting. We don't have to pay the bills and balance the checkbook. We can do what we want.

MARGIE: I happen to be a crackerjack checkbook balancer.

LOUIS: I bet.

(Silence)

MARGIE: I miss you.

LOUIS: I'm here now.

MARGIE: If you could be anywhere in the world you wanted to be, where would it be?

LOUIS: Here. Now.

MARGIE: I didn't ask with whom. I said "where". I'd pick Australia.

(Pause. LOUIS doesn't offer an answer.)

MARGIE: Where would you pick?

LOUIS: I'd pick...you know, I'm getting hungry... New York. There's this little place in the village, has the most incredible food. The hell with all the sunshine. No one can cook out here!

MARGIE: I cook.

LOUIS: I don't need you to cook.

MARGIE: But I like to. I've asked you over.

LOUIS: Marge...

MARGIE: Last Christmas I did. I put up a tree and I asked you over. I even bought eggnog. *(Pause)* I heard the Hotel has a dynamite Sunday Brunch. All the champagne you can swallow.

LOUIS: Yeah?

MARGIE: And we can go up to Hoover Dam afterward. It's the biggest in the country.

LOUIS: Grand Coolee is I think.

MARGIE: Oh.

LOUIS: Yeah.

MARGIE: Second biggest.

(Silence)

LOUIS: I can't. I have something to tell you. I feel really shitty about it, but I might as well say it. *(Pause)* I may have to leave a little early. My kid has a soccer game.

MARGIE: You're joking.

LOUIS: Would I joke about a kid's soccer game? He's the star of the whole damn team. These are the playoffs. They just made the playoffs this afternoon. That's why I was late in the first place.

MARGIE: And in the second place...?

LOUIS: Well how the hell am I supposed to know they'd win ten straight? Look, I know you're angry and disappointed.

MARGIE: Don't tell me what I am. I'll choose the words for what I am. *(Picking the cover off the dish on the serving cart)* Care for a turkey club? *(Starting to pick at the turkey club)*

LOUIS: Margie, he's only a little kid. The game's first thing Sunday morning. Jesus, I can't miss it. Come on, we're going downstairs to hear Sinatra, order a nice dinner, then we'll come back and get into bed. We've got tomorrow night and you can stay as long as you want. The room's all paid for. There's an indoor pool and sauna. You can order up breakfast in bed Sunday. Wait a minute. We can order it up—early—together.

MARGIE: How early?

LOUIS: My flight's at eight.

MARGIE: I thought you said "may" have to leave early.

LOUIS: I meant "have" to. I am really sorry. *(He now nervously bites into the turkey club.)*

MARGIE: You don't "have" to.

LOUIS: You don't have kids, so you don't know.

MARGIE: *That is correct.*

LOUIS: We can have breakfast at six-thirty.

MARGIE: I'm not hungry that early.

LOUIS: How do you know how you'll be then? We can do everything we were going to do.

MARGIE: Just do it fast, in double time.

(Still picking at the turkey club, together with LOUIS)

MARGIE: The turkey tastes exactly like rattlesnake, which is indigenous to the area. *(Pause)* I don't think this is going to be such a wonderful weekend, Louis. Why can't the nanny take him to the game?

LOUIS: They don't do that kind of thing. *(Pause)* I mean you're lucky I even got here at all.

MARGIE: Lucky me!

LOUIS: I'm sorry. I didn't mean that. Look, my wife's plane was taking off for New York, then I had to come back into town for the game, then back out again to the airport...that's for starters.

MARGIE: You make it sound like hardship duty.

LOUIS: I'm saying it wasn't a snap.

MARGIE: If you don't want to be here with me...

LOUIS: No, I do. I'm just having two emotions at once. Okay?

MARGIE: It's called ambivalence. *(Pause)* Do you and Isobel make love?

LOUIS: I don't think I'm going to answer that.

MARGIE: Tell me.

LOUIS: Every Saturday night. I don't want to talk about her with you, Margie.

MARGIE: You wouldn't risk that.

LOUIS: You're going to ruin it.

MARGIE: What's *it*?

LOUIS: You know.

MARGIE: No.

LOUIS: I don't have to say.

MARGIE: Let's hear it for the mighty unspoken word! Keep it pretty. Keep it wrapped up. I can take a hint. No, I can take a command. "Lay off what's not yours." Then what is? What's my location? Where do I stand? You were once a film director; you understand *location*. If you want to get there, you better tell me where I am. It always helps to know where you are.

LOUIS: It's *just* a small change of plan.

MARGIE: Then what *is* the plan? It's not that I'm not flexible. *(Pause)* If you got married again, would you have children?

LOUIS: *(Interrupting)* No one said anything about getting married again.

MARGIE: *I did.*

LOUIS: No promises here.

MARGIE: I'm talking "in general". Would you like more children? Some people take joy in multiplying.

LOUIS: Two's just right. One's up in the attic and we're sending the second one up in the spring, which will give us the entire second floor and a little privacy.

MARGIE: So you can make love more than once a week.

LOUIS: That's one of the possibilities. Come over here and stop asking so many questions to which I don't think you want to hear the answers.

MARGIE: No. I *want* answers. That's what I *want.*

LOUIS: I think you need a hug. *(Coming over and holding her)*

MARGIE: I think I need more than a hug. *(Breaking away)*

LOUIS: What the hell *do* you want? This is starting to feel like an impacted wisdom tooth.

MARGIE: You're getting angry.

LOUIS: I'm not... I am.

MARGIE: I think a family's important.

LOUIS: Not as important as it used to be.

MARGIE: You say that because you have one.

LOUIS: You are coming on like a Mack truck. We came here to relax and here we are in this suite which costs a hundred dollars a day, talking about I don't know what, and I don't know how that happened.

MARGIE: You're saying let's talk about pleasant things.

LOUIS: I don't want to *talk.* I'd like to go downstairs and *eat* and *hear* Sinatra and *come* upstairs and try out the sheets.

MARGIE: You don't want to talk about feelings.

LOUIS: Maybe I'm not always feeling. *(Pause)* I want to go down and see Sinatra.

MARGIE: What I'm actually afraid of is getting old alone. *(Pause)* Well I don't hear any offers.

LOUIS: I'm not missing Sinatra, Margie.

MARGIE: What I want is to be connected to something in the universe.

LOUIS: What are you talking about? When you start with this philosophic shit, I don't know what you're saying—

MARGIE: It is not shit because I'm saying I want you. I mean it must not be news that my Retirement Plan does not give me that thrill! My menu of corporate perks, in fact, depresses me. They send it once a year; I read it sometimes in the bathroom.

LOUIS: You're looking to the wrong man. I'm more screwed up than anyone.

MARGIE: Do you forget about me at night when you go home?

LOUIS: No.

MARGIE: When do you think about me?

LOUIS: In the shower, sometimes sitting at the breakfast table. Why is this coming up suddenly?

MARGIE: Even when Isobel's there?

LOUIS: Yes... Lying in bed at night waiting to fall asleep.

MARGIE: Do you know the windmill you brought me back from Greece? I have it by my bed.

LOUIS: That's good. I'm glad you like it.

MARGIE: No. I dropped it and one of the sails broke off.

LOUIS: That's too bad. If I ever go back to Greece again I'll get you another one.

MARGIE: *(Pause)* I bet when you do it it's better with me.

LOUIS: It's always good at the beginning of anything.

MARGIE: Does Isobel know about me?

LOUIS: *(Pause)* She found a card you sent me in my briefcase. I said it was from one of the girls at work.

MARGIE: Thanks.

LOUIS: Well that's the truth.

MARGIE: You could lie a little. *(Pauses, angrily)* I'm a department manager.

LOUIS: I stand corrected.

MARGIE: *(Pause)* This Christmas I will *not* plan to buy eggnog and sit home and wait for you....

LOUIS: You're just feeling blue 'cause the holidays are coming.

MARGIE: Wrong.

LOUIS: Then let it go.

MARGIE: No! I've been watching it *go*. So maybe it is the holidays, it's our anniversary, the constellations are in the right place in the sky. *You're* late, *I'm* late, *it's* late! I want to be *first, primary, right up there!* Top of the line! You know me! I have an image to keep up. I was the best where I came from. I was Miss St. Louis. I had a crown and an evening gown and I rode through downtown on the back of a white Cadillac convertible with the *Lieu*tenant Governor. The Governor was away down at Willow Springs at the time. Just had a tornado, flattened out the town. Dead, flat... I want to be the best, Louis. Your best girl... Stringtime's over. It's so hard to keep the act fresh. *(Beat)* It's an old rule in the Midwest you gotta dance with the girl what brung you.

LOUIS: I came to get away, but I feel like I'm in the thick of it... A good dinner, some nice wine, Sinatra and satin sheets, or I don't know, 'cause we're getting into an awful lot of stuff here tonight. *(Standing up, making moves to get dressed to go out)*

MARGIE: Okay! Forget it! Let's talk about important things. Did you see the sunset tonight?

LOUIS: I saw it from the plane. The sky was all orange.

MARGIE: It wasn't orange! It was pink! Pink! It was so pretty it almost made me cry. *(Pause)* Louis, you're the only man I've met in the last couple of years who I liked, who liked me too. I don't know what's wrong with me. I think I'm pretty. Don't you think I'm pretty, Louis?

LOUIS: You know you are.

MARGIE: If I knew, would I be asking? I'll be thirty-eight next Wednesday. Happy Birthday to me. I better say it out loud, because I *am*. And nothing belongs to me. If I made out my will, what would I leave? My cat? My stereo? My ficus tree? If I was in a serious accident, who are they supposed to call? My mother in her nursing home? My Aunt Grace down in Florida?

LOUIS: They could call me.

MARGIE: That's not the point.

LOUIS: What *is* the point, Margie? *(Silence)* I'm very involved with my family and will be for a long time.

MARGIE: I haven't got that long.

LOUIS: I thought I made that clear.

MARGIE: As crystal. *(Pause)* We'll have to go, you said once, on a real vacation, some place neither of us has been. I've never been to Italy. Someone told me if you go anywhere, don't miss Venice or Sienna.

LOUIS: I've been to Sienna.

MARGIE: Then it's clearly Venice.

LOUIS: Clearly.

MARGIE: Because no one should go away empty-handed.

LOUIS: No.

MARGIE: Clearly. *(Pause)* So, maybe it's now or never on having a baby, and since we were planning on fucking anyway—I mean why else come to a hotel? Certainly not for the color television. So I want to ask you...this is really impossible to spit out. *(Taking a breath)* I'd like you to have a baby with me.

LOUIS: What?

MARGIE: A baby. Well I can't do it by myself! *(Angrily)* I would if I could. Don't stare at me!

LOUIS: What is this?

MARGIE: I told you! I'm tired of being alone! *(Pause)* When I go home at night I open all the windows in the apartment to let some noise in. All I'm asking for is your sperm. We all know how you love sex. *(Starting to break down)* You told me it's your only pleasure. Didn't you? *(Pause)* I'll even sign a document releasing you from responsibility.

LOUIS: I like you a lot, Margie. In the office, some days, I can't stop looking at you.

MARGIE: Answer me, Louis.

LOUIS: But I'm no connection with any universe. *(Pause)* Meet me in the Riviera Room in fifteen minutes, and we can go back to the beginning? *(Picking up his suit jacket)*

MARGIE: I think you're very handsome, especially your eyes. *(Pause, no response)* Please...

LOUIS: I'm already taken.

MARGIE: Well I'm not.

LOUIS: Yes. I know.

(Lights fade.)

(End of scene)

END OF ACT ONE

ACT TWO

Scene One

(Time: Same evening. One hour later.)

(Place: The Birdcage Bar. FELIX is behind the bar. ALMA sits at the bar with a drink, eating peanuts, which are set out. Recorded music plays in the background.)

FELIX: Looks like a washout to me, Alma. Almost eleven, and Sinatra has not come out of his room. Someone said he's hurt bad in the eye. Some waiter threw a tray at it. Maybe he got rude. He sometimes gets rude according to the magazines. Maybe one of his bodyguards got rude. He has three bodyguards.

ALMA: That's a lot of guards for one body.

FELIX: He's tying up the whole kitchen. He ordered pineapple for breakfast—fresh pineapple. Well we don't have pineapple. So we offer him strawberries. Well he doesn't want strawberries. But I don't blame him, 'cause where does a strawberry come to a pineapple.

ALMA: Another vodka.

FELIX: Right. *(Making it)* But he can strum the nerve endings of a ballad like nobody else. Last year, he's here, the whole audience is sobbing. Grown women. Tell you what he's got. Passion. How old's the man? Still running on passion.

ALMA: Good for Sinatra.

FELIX: You lead with your heart, you can't go wrong.

ALMA: My friend's friend came back.

FELIX: I think you should try the slot machines.

ALMA: I just did. Fourteen of them. *(Shaking her head)* I don't trust my luck anymore tonight.

FELIX: Then you're in the wrong place.

ALMA: I'm always in the wrong place. My timing seems to be terribly off.

(Sound of noise from a nearby lounge)

FELIX: They're going crazy out there. Whole hotel's in the Ballroom waiting, which means no wonder everything's berserk, seeing "Action" is this place's middle name. So I say you want peace and quiet, go stand in a cornfield in Iowa. Come on. Whaddaya say? Whaddaya say? Cheer up and play!

(ALMA *nods her head indifferently and* FELIX *goes over to her*)

FELIX: Hey, Tokyo Alma, how would you like to get in to see Sinatra? Bet I could squeeze you in.

ALMA: Make room and I'll love you forever and a day.

FELIX: Good, because we like to keep the customers satisfied.

(LOUIS *enters the Bar*)

LOUIS: Dewar's double, on the rocks... (*Staring at* ALMA)

FELIX: You come to see Sinatra? Fair warning. Folks say he may adiose. The Cage heard it was a bomb scare. The Bar's the last to know. You with the group from Texas?

LOUIS: Yes.

FELIX: That's funny. You don't look like you're with the group from Texas. (*Noise is getting louder*) People sound like they're getting mad. They're yelling for their money back. Management will offer rainchecks. Some rainy day if Sinatra doesn't show.

ALMA: Frank Sinatra sure caused a lot of problems here tonight.

LOUIS: Among other trouble makers. Thanks, lady, for sending me on a wild goose chase.

ALMA: She wasn't there, huh?

LOUIS: No.

ALMA: Dumb Alma.

LOUIS: But I found her.

ALMA: Then I'm happy for you.

(*Noise O S*)

FELIX: Listen to them out there. Why do people gotta behave like animals?

LOUIS: The dining room's a mausoleum. The crowd's all out there waiting for Sinatra.

FELIX: This could turn out to be something big if old blue eyes doesn't sing tonight. We could all be singing for our supper. 'Cause hell, if Vegas ever blows, there blows the world. (*To* ALMA) But *if* Sinatra *shows* and *blows* his horn... (*Pointing to* ALMA)

ALMA: And I'm going to be here to hear it.

FELIX: Leave it to me to charm the maitre d' into a fallen ticket. (*To* ALMA) Don't give anything away.

(FELIX *goes to the house phone. The lights fade down on him and up on* ALMA *and* LOUIS.)

ALMA: I bet they get a substitute. It would have to be some substitute. Maybe they'll get Dean Martin.

LOUIS: He's dead. He died a couple of years ago.

ALMA: God, if you don't read the papers every day.

LOUIS: El Dino is dead.

ALMA: He must have died while I was in Tokyo. Everyone died while I was in Tokyo. My husband's in the Army. He's a captain.

LOUIS: *(Saluting)* I salute you then.

ALMA: No. He's the Captain. I'm just his wife. Are you married?

LOUIS: Kind of.

ALMA: Well either you are or you aren't.

LOUIS: *(Helping himself to another drink)* Yes I am.

ALMA: So what are you doing here meeting my friend Margie Hammersmith?

LOUIS: That's my business.

ALMA: It certainly is.

LOUIS: Why did you send me away before?

ALMA: That's my business.

LOUIS: It certainly is.

ALMA: Because I was there first.

(*Music comes on the jukebox—Sinatra—"My Favorite Year". Pause*)

ALMA: That is my favorite song.

LOUIS: Mine too. I don't think it was nice.

ALMA: I don't think so either. I lost my head. I sometimes do. Only I always find it, usually.

(*Pause*)

LOUIS: Would you like to dance?

ALMA: With you?

LOUIS: Seeing it's your favorite song.

ALMA: I've been married twelve years. I have two children, but one of them's dyslexic. He can't read straight. I'm separated—just.

LOUIS: Maybe you'll get back together again. Let's dance.

(They begin to dance, dancing closely. ALMA *hums to the music.)*

ALMA: I don't think so.

LOUIS: You're a sexy lady.

ALMA: I am?

LOUIS: Yes.

ALMA: What makes you say I'm sexy?

(They are dancing closely, not looking at one another.)

LOUIS: I can always tell by the eyes. Big brown eyes.

ALMA: They're blue.

LOUIS: *(Not skipping a beat, continuing to dance)* Big blue eyes.

ALMA: What else?

LOUIS: What?

ALMA: Is sexy?

LOUIS: The way you move.

ALMA: Yeah?

LOUIS: Yeah.

ALMA: I never thought about that. I just move.

LOUIS: Well you move good.

ALMA: Really?

LOUIS: Really. Got a nice body.

ALMA: Oh you think so? Be honest.

LOUIS: You're asking me, I'm telling you.

ALMA: I was worried I didn't have it. Because if no one says it to you and you're the only one who thinks so, that's not a big vote.

LOUIS: Well you have a very nice body.

ALMA: Thank you.

(They continue to dance.)

ALMA: My husband's name is Malcolm and I wouldn't take him back for all the tea in Japan.

LOUIS: Let's just dance.

ALMA: It's a crazy place, Las Vegas. No warmth. It's the kind of place that makes you miss your kids. I miss my kids. I miss my husband. You should see his face... soft all over and he's turning gray now, but nice, and he let his hair grow long and he has ridges in his back. It's hard to explain. At night, when we used to fall asleep, he always put his leg over mine.

LOUIS: Well that's nice. He sounds nice. Do you have a room?

ALMA: I was looking for something. Do you have kids?

LOUIS: I have an English sheepdog who's a lot of trouble, and two boys, top athletes, both of them.

ALMA: Oh I think it's nice to be athletic in this country. For one thing, it's expected. My kids Judy and Jimmy are good kids; they're decent, which I think is the most important.

LOUIS: If you want to be with your kids so badly, why don't you go back to Japan?

ALMA: Because I will, dum dum. (Beat) He bought me a new coat and this silk blouse I'm wearing. I mean he was kind. The children were both crying. I told them I'd come back. I didn't have to leave exactly, but what was I supposed to do by myself all separated in Japan and no finances? At least I have relatives, like I have a sister in San Francisco. I think I'm a good person. What he said was that he'd fallen in love with someone else. I think it's dangerous to live only by your passions, don't you? Because there's such a thing as right and wrong, a code of living.

LOUIS: He sounds like a bastard.

ALMA: Oh Malcolm's just an opportunist. Well live and learn. People say he's a looker, kind of a cross between Robert Redford and Billy Crystal.

LOUIS: Do you want to spend the night together? I'd like to make love to you.

ALMA: (Pause) What's your wife's name?

LOUIS: Come on.

ALMA: What's her name?

LOUIS: Isobel.

ALMA: Is she decent?

LOUIS: Absolutely.

ALMA: Do you love her?

LOUIS: (Pause) Maybe...I don't know.

ALMA: Does she know that?

LOUIS: That's why she went to New York.

ALMA: Are you in love with my friend, Margie Hammersmith?

LOUIS: I don't know. Yes or no, Alma? We could just lie together. (Pause) Don't make me beg. I like you. You're got a pretty face and you're lively.

ALMA: My husband called me sunshine...but I was looking for something more permanent.

LOUIS: Oh Alma, pretty Alma, if you were my girl I would buy you a condo on the beach at Malibu where the real estate's going nowhere but up. Come on...give me a hug...just a hug...I need a hug.

ALMA: *(Sharp and straight)* I need enough to get to St Louis. Two hundred and sixty-eight dollars one way, American Airlines.

LOUIS: No fooling around with you.

ALMA: I may be separated and scared a lot about money and things like growing old, but one thing about me, I've got my dignity. And I would like the loan of the money, 'cause I know you've got it, and I am really desperate, and I'll pay you back when I get it, and I will not lie down with you, 'cause I don't even know you, and afterwards you would blow away like a white puff dandelion. And please hurry before I change my mind. But before you go, I would give you a hug, so come here and let me hold you.... Come on.

(ALMA embraces him.)

LOUIS: You're turning me down.

ALMA: It's the spirit of the times. Maybe it's catchy. Maybe you shouldn't let me hold you so tight.

(FELIX enters while ALMA and LOUIS are embracing. ALMA sees FELIX and runs out of the bar.)

LOUIS: Women!

FELIX: Love 'em.

LOUIS: I've been trying. *(Pushing his glass towards FELIX)* Fill her up.

FELIX: What happened to your girlfriend? *(Making the drink, giving it to LOUIS)*

LOUIS: *(Pause)* She had a machine gun. What's the word on Sinatra?

FELIX: Looks like a washout. He hasn't come out of his room. People aren't even sure he's in there anymore.

LOUIS: Hell, I came to see Sinatra.

FELIX: I came because they told me there was gold out here in the hills. Bet you my Ford Taurus you're not going to get what you came here for. You a betting man?

LOUIS: Fourteen years with the same barber, twelve years with the same wife. And thanks, but I have two cars that are always in the shop. *(Pause)* If a woman asked you to have a baby with her, what would you say?

FELIX: Buy a dog. It's cheaper. Two hundred thousand bucks today, according to *Time* magazine to bring up a human person.

LOUIS: I'm serious. If someone really asked you that.

FELIX: I would run very fast.

LOUIS: She's gone nuts! She's acting like my wife or something! She asked me to have a baby with her!

FELIX: *(Beat)* She was probably kidding. *(Beat)* Which one?

LOUIS: The one I'm with.

FELIX: At least she was polite to ask.

LOUIS: They start mixing in serious things like kids. Hey.

FELIX: My mother had me and stopped. She couldn't find my father to do it again.

LOUIS: And this has been a dynamite romance.

FELIX: I'd stand in, but I don't think she'd want me. Looks like they're all after you.

LOUIS: Oh sure, one for the money, and one for the kid.

FELIX: But come on. A woman wants you, wants your kid? That's wholesome! That's damn Norman Rockwell American! All they ever want here is screwing, and fast, so they can get back to the tables, or back to sleep, or back at their husbands or wives or lovers, or the best fuck, fuck and forget...F & F.

LOUIS: I wish I stayed home and pruned the azalea bushes. This place is sordid.

FELIX: I wished I stayed in Brooklyn, New York, where the dirt's obvious.

LOUIS: I'm a good family man.

FELIX: Well definitions are changing quick in this country.

LOUIS: When I was a kid, you'd wake up, first thing you'd hear, birds singing in the morning.

FELIX: The longer you stay here, the less chance you have of winning. The house percentages are always working against you. Sinatra or not, if I was you, I would not get mixed up with those young ladies up there who are mixed up as it is, and I would leave them for me. I mean there's only so much apple pie to go around in this country. You got your piece, like it or not.

LOUIS: Felix, bet you a ride to the airport in your Ford someone here's going to get what they asked for. *(Pause)* I was always a fucker for happy endings.

(LOUIS pushes his glass towards FELIX as the lights fade.)

(End of scene)

Scene Two

(Time: Half an hour later)

(Place: The hotel suite. MARGIE sits on the couch in her bathrobe, an open pizza box in front of her. She takes the last piece. The T V is on. An old movie is playing.)

VOICE FROM THE T V: *(Dialogue from a classic scene in American film, Casablanca.)* "I came to Casablanca for the waters." "The waters? What waters? We're in the desert." "I was misinformed."

(There is a knock at the door,)

MARGIE: *(Turning off the T V and walking to the door)* Coming! *(At the door)* Yes?

ALMA: *(O S)* It's me, Alma.

MARGIE: *(Opening the door)* It's you.

ALMA: It's me. I wanted to see what developed or didn't, and 'cause my bags are here. *(Looking around)* I see you had a pizza.

MARGIE: That's what you see.

ALMA: *(Looking at the box)* I always order extra cheese. They do that for extra money. In Japan anchovy pizza's very popular because of it being on the ocean. I never knew anchovy was a fish. I always thought it was like an olive.

MARGIE: It's a small salty fish.

(Pause)

ALMA: Guess what? Sinatra may be canceled.

MARGIE: Whoop whoop adoo!

ALMA: You look terrible. You've been crying. Have you been crying?

MARGIE: Yes.

ALMA: You want me to stay?

MARGIE: You can stay if you want.

ALMA: Only if you want.

MARGIE: I said it's okay.

ALMA: Okay, then I'll stay. *(Picking at the leftover cheese stuck to the roof of the pizza box)*

MARGIE: But I'm warning you, I'm not sleepy.

ALMA: Oh Las Vegas is no place to sleep. Live, live, live!

MARGIE: And he may be back.

ALMA: How did your meeting go?

(Pause)

MARGIE: Poorly. It sucked. The minute you ask for something, they leave.

ALMA: Once I asked Malcolm for a diamond ring, seeing he never gave me one when we got married and diamonds are cheap in Japan too and you could even get one at the P X. I asked him for pear shaped. Don't you think round's boring? *(Pause)* What did you ask him for? What you said before? *(Humming the first bar of "Here Comes the Bride")*

MARGIE: That's private between us.

ALMA: I'm sorry. I intruded.

MARGIE: You didn't because I didn't tell you.

ALMA: You still got my turkey club?

MARGIE: I put it out the door.

ALMA: That's okay. I got some peanuts down in the bar. *(Opening the door a crack, peeking out, then closing it)* Gone! Boy, you must have really done something to have him leave, after he had so much trouble getting here.

MARGIE: I put it to him. Maybe if I put it better... *(Starting to pack furiously)*

ALMA: I was thinking on the plane over, maybe if I would have dressed sexier or put on makeup, you know, when he came home, just like the women's magazines tell you, though I did some nights, just not *every* night. Then I thought to myself, how come *me*? I mean he had this terrible acne and he never put on any lotions, just walked around with all these pimples. He called them eruptions like he was a famous volcano or something.

MARGIE: The point is, I'm not asking anyone for anything again. Next time if I want it, I'll take it. *(Pointing to the picture on the hotel wall)* I think it is so boring that every hotel room in America has a picture of Picasso's Don Quixote on the wall. He chased windmills and we're chasing men.

ALMA: I'm not chasing anyone.

MARGIE: We can't catch them anyway.

ALMA: God, some women can pick men up, they have this knack. But they say if you're desperate, men pick that right up. *(Beat)* Anyway, it's a trial separation. How come you're packing?

MARGIE: No reason to stay. On to greener fields, but you can stay if you like. The room's paid in full 'til Sunday. When's your flight?

ALMA: I don't know exactly yet. *(Beat)* Did your boyfriend leave because you asked him to marry you?

MARGIE: Louis is a V I P in the record industry, not my boyfriend.

ALMA: But he said no.

MARGIE: Yes, he said no! Alma, you're a pain in the ass!

ALMA: I'm just trying hard to be your friend.

MARGIE: Well the last thing I need tonight is a friend! *(Beat)* I'm sorry. I didn't mean that. And I didn't ask him to marry me.

ALMA: Good.

MARGIE: Something stupider. I asked him to have a baby with me.

ALMA: You're kidding!

MARGIE: Here I am, I've been plotting this whole thing out and I'm losing my lead time, and people are saying, "*Give* it to him, *get* him against the wall". And experts keep saying—they had this program on the *Today* program—"After forty, it's dicey".

ALMA: Which is crummy because it takes that long to grow up to be anybody's mother.

MARGIE: And the idea of the baby just came to me.

ALMA: Look, it just happened to me. I didn't even think about it. Here you really wanted to do it.

MARGIE: I would do better to go to some lab and use a test tube...but I know Louis and he has good features and he's bright. He told me his I Q and I couldn't believe it.

ALMA: ...And anyway... you were in love with him.

(Pause)

MARGIE: *(Realizing for the first time)* Yeah.

ALMA: Yeah.

MARGIE: Damn. Damn. DAMN! DAMN! DAMN!

ALMA: He's a jerk for turning you down. A beautiful woman like you.

MARGIE: He must have been blinded by my beauty. *(Beat)* For the first time, Alma, I have no clear plan.

ALMA: *(Pause)* If I ever see him again, I would wallop him.

MARGIE: Screw him!

(ALMA shrugs her shoulders. The two giggle.)

MARGIE: Yeah. Maybe.

ALMA: Kids are a royal pain anyway. They're always going through stages that are impossible. No one else would even live with them, except their own parents, who are stuck for life. It's like putting a cake in the oven. You do everything, but you don't know until you open the door how it's going to turn out. The whole thing can fall in without anyone even making a loud noise. You could spend your whole life whispering and the whole thing could still fall in.

MARGIE: Thank you, Alma, but I don't believe a word of it. *(Looking out the window)* God, it's almost midnight and every light is lit. No one's gone to sleep.

ALMA: I guess that's what you do in Las Vegas, or don't do.

MARGIE: *(Looking out the window)* Look at that billboard flashing on and off. As much energy up there as in the whole sky. *(Reading)* "FRANK SINATRA APPEARING TONIGHT" *(Pause)* Sold out.

ALMA: He sure sings a crock.

MARGIE: And we bought it.

ALMA: Want to know the most beautiful thing Malcolm ever did, the thing that made me feel the bears would never come in the night and eat me to pieces? He kissed me on the forehead when he went to say goodnight that first winter I met him. I could feel that kiss on my forehead. I still can. It was sweet. Most men are afraid to be sweet.

MARGIE: They think we want to be ravished, taken over like the Americans marching into Paris, marching through the arch.

ALMA: I'm scared, Margie. I don't know of what.

MARGIE: Nothing to be scared about. Look at all the stars hanging out there in the sky. Look at all the company we've got. They've been there so long, alone, like the earth, or clustered in galaxies, some fixed, Alma, some traveling. They've seen everything, watched us connecting, disconnecting, and finally, like them, burning out, running clear out of energy. *(Pause)* But that takes millions of years, the birth and death of stars. *(Pause)* If we stand very still we can see ourselves in their reflection.

ALMA: I just didn't know all this was going to happen. My boy's dyslexic.

MARGIE: You told me.

ALMA: I didn't know that was going to happen.

MARGIE: I know you didn't.

ALMA: Or that I wouldn't be married and I'd be wandering around the country looking for a place to lie down my head so it could stop spinning.

MARGIE: I bet your boy will grow up just fine.

ALMA: You think so?

MARGIE: Oh kids are amazing. I know this girl, she was born all uncoordinated and funny, everything just hung in a funny way, but she was determined to conquer it, so she worked out every day until she was such an outstanding gymnast, you wouldn't believe it. Last I heard she was over in Europe in the Olympics and then she went on to be a coach for other kids.

ALMA: You mean Gemma Simeone?

MARGIE: Gemma. Right.

ALMA: She's dead Margie.

MARGIE: No. She's coaching kids for the Olympics.

ALMA: Her mother wrote to me last Christmas when I sent her a Christmas card. She died the Christmas before.

MARGIE: That's terrible. I was trying to tell you this good story.

ALMA: You remember Freddie Duncan?

MARGIE: Big tall guy.

ALMA: Well Gemma was always secretly in love with him. She always wanted a date with Freddie Duncan.

MARGIE: He had a funny face but a nice body.

ALMA: That's him. Well that Christmas she came home, he came home. He was married now and divorced, but Gemma was still unattached. So he asked her out to this Christmas party. Gemma was naturally all excited. Her brother, who I wrote to, said she got this new dress, which was a big deal, since she hardly ever wore dresses because she didn't feel feminine, which I don't understand since she certainly was, but this spurred her all up and she got this green velvet dress. He brother said she looked like a princess in it. Well Freddie came to pick her up and he'd been drinking.

MARGIE: Freddie Duncan was always a big drinker.

ALMA: Well people don't change, and off they go in his little red Corvette. He had a couple of drinks more at the party, I guess, and they were on their way home, and it was now pretty late, and maybe he took her parking—

MARGIE: To see the submarine races.

ALMA: (*Excited that* MARGIE *remembers anything*) Only the car slipped... it was raining...and Gemma got killed and Freddie's in a nursing home. He's a vegetable. (*Beat*) So Gemma got her date with Freddie.

MARGIE: That's a terrible story, Alma.

ALMA: I'm beginning to think it doesn't go easy for anybody. I'm scared to visit my mother's grave, Margie. I don't want to look.

MARGIE: Just do it. March one foot in front of the other.

ALMA: Maybe I'll take a taxi out, like I saw in this movie once, and the driver sits and waits for you. There's no stone yet, but I'm gonna offer to chip in with my sister. And I may even write to Malcolm. Malcolm was very fond of my mother.

MARGIE: Tell you what. You tell me when you're going to go, the exact time, and wherever I am, I'll stop what I'm doing and be there with you. I'll transmit my spirit right across the Continental Divide.

ALMA: Hey... Hey, Margie...we're getting to be good friends again.

MARGIE: Or maybe for the first time.

ALMA: (Making a Girl Scout salute, signing) Make new friends, But keep the old, One is silver, And the other gold.

MARGIE: (Putting her fingers to ALMA's lips) Don't. It will make it go away.

ALMA: Right this minute my cup runneth over. Usually when that happens I manage to spill it.

MARGIE: Alma, I've come to an important conclusion here tonight. They are never going to make the dream come true. John Wayne whispering "I will build you a house in the bend of the river where the cottonweed grows, Nellie". (Pause) I bet he didn't even know how to build a house. I bet he was scared crazy.

ALMA: Oh not John Wayne. He was never scared.

MARGIE: I don't know what's so wonderful about men in the first place. Just sex. That's the only difference. (Pause)

ALMA: That's some difference. Well, sex isn't the end of the world.

MARGIE: The only thing that's the end of the world...

ALMA: Is the end of the world. Look at Margaret Mead. Was she thinking about sex all the time? And you want to look at what she accomplished. Madame Curie. Did you see her sitting home with a lot of little Curies? Barbara Bush. I don't think she was sitting around the White House thinking about sex all the time.

MARGIE: Amelia Earhart.

ALMA: Coretta King.

MARGIE: Jackie Kennedy.

ALMA: Oh no. I don't think we should put her on the list.

MARGIE: Eleanor Roosevelt then.

ALMA: A prime example. She wasn't waiting for any Prince to come riding up the highway. I bet she slept good at night. We're just afraid to be free. I mean what's the Statue of Liberty standing out there in the harbor of New York for? Her good health?

MARGIE: Alma, I propose we celebrate, that we have a midnight champagne breakfast.

ALMA: That's a classy idea and it would also taste good.

MARGIE: In honor of our meeting in the middle of nowhere.

ALMA: On our way to somewhere, maybe.

MARGIE: *(Picking up room service menu)* We'll start with a bottle of their best. Imported. Hey. I don't see the domestic giving us such a thrill. Then on to the juice and eggs... *(Moving towards the phone)*

ALMA: And bacon! Bacon!

MARGIE: We'll order whatever we want. The way I see it, M G M owes it to us for all the bunk they brought us, including Louis.

ALMA: *Ah, Men!*

MARGIE: *(Into the phone)* Room Service. Room 1222. A couple of bottles of very good French champagne, four eggs, once over light...

ALMA: *(Over* MARGIE's *phone conversation)* Can we have sunny side up?

MARGIE: *(Into the phone)* Sunny side up.

ALMA: The two O Js should be fresh squeezed.

MARGIE: *(Into the phone)* Two O Js fresh.

ALMA: *(While* MARGIE *is giving the order)* And prune Danish. I am crazy for prune Danish.

MARGIE: *(Into the phone)* Prune Danish, and coffee.

ALMA: And bacon...don't forget the bacon.

MARGIE: *(Into the phone)* A *large* order of bacon. *(Hanging up the phone)*

ALMA: I haven't had champagne since my wedding. They don't do it so much in Japan. Oh God, they don't do a lot of things in Japan.

MARGIE: Welcome home then, and you better be hungry!

ALMA: I think when I visit the grave, you know what? I'm going to plant little lilacs all around it. My mother loved lilacs. *(Beat)* Margie, I have something to tell you and it's something awful. *(Going right on, speaking quickly, as to get the information spit out)* Before, in the bar, when you went out to call Louis, he came and I told him you weren't there, that you went to the airport.

MARGIE: You told him I went to the airport?

*(*ALMA *nods her head.)*

MARGIE: Why did you do a thing like that?

ALMA: I guess I didn't want to be alone. *(Pause)* I'm sorry.

MARGIE: *Sorry?* You ruined my entire evening! My entire weekend!

ALMA: My whole like was falling apart. I wanted to get you for my friend.

MARGIE: Falling apart? My life is probably decimated because of you. By the time he came he was in such a mood.

ALMA: Don't blame it all on me. *(Beat)* Just sometimes the words come out of my tongue before I get a chance to circulate them around my head. Especially when I want something.

MARGIE: Well, next time, Alma, when you want something, *(Imitating the circular motion ALMA has just made)* first circulate.

ALMA: Okay, so I'm sorry. He's not worth scratching over.

MARGIE: It's a question of integrity.

ALMA: Well you know, if it's such a big question of integrity, how come when I really needed an old friend, you dumped me one-two-three when he called back and said he was coming?

MARGIE: *(Interrupting angrily)* I am NOT an old friend! I am an acquaintance! I was a classmate!

(Now shouting at each other)

ALMA: But you're not a stranger! You know my name! You know my mother!

MARGIE: I met her once!

ALMA: So we're not strangers then. I'm here with seventy-eight dollars in my purse which is what I had left out of my grocery money. He got me the ticket to California because I said that's all I wanted and I would stay with my sister, but you can't stay where nobody wants you. I have my pride. I'm not going to get down and beg.

MARGIE: You could have told me you had no money!

ALMA: See, Malcolm dumped me, because I didn't turn him on, he said, and after he told me that, well I wouldn't make love to him anymore. Well I couldn't and that's what you call my integrity. I've never been so near the bottom in my whole life, and then I see you before, downstairs. Oh God, I could've kissed the sight of you.

MARGIE: I though you almost didn't say "hello".

ALMA: Oh that was just a fat lie.

MARGIE: Which you're evidently a pro at. How dare you send Louis away. He was mine!

ALMA: I didn't sleep with him!

MARGIE: *(Sarcastically)* Good for you!

(Silence)

ALMA: I was loyal to you even though I was sorely tempted.

MARGIE: I wasn't aware that you were being deluged with offers.

ALMA: You were mean to me all in the hopes of a stupid fuck!

MARGIE: Alma, shut up!

ALMA: Wanna hear an old Army joke?

MARGIE: No, I do not want to hear an old Army joke.

ALMA: I saw your lover down in the bar before and he asked me to go to bed with him. Said I was sexy...I'm sorry.

MARGIE: *(Pause, then coolly)* He was no doubt drunk.

ALMA: I think he was very sober. The joke's on us, Margie, fighting over such a rinky-dink trophy.

MARGIE: That trophy is the only real trophy, for your information, I have won since I won the girl with the most school spirit, which I only got because I could jump higher than the other cheerleaders, which only shows to go, how high I would jump through anyone's hoop to get applause.

ALMA: He's married anyway. He has two kids.

MARGIE: That's right. I've got the point. I know the point. It's sticking right in my throat! Don't choke me on the point! *(Beat)* Some days, Alma, I can't stand myself or anyone else. *(Beat)* The pickings are slim out there over thirty. *(Pause)* I'm telling you. You'll see. And I'm not throwing the idea out the window of having something—a guy, a baby, I don't know what....

ALMA: Well no one said to stop looking, because, like in the desert, the bus driver was telling me, there's aren't any seasons. It only blooms when it *happens* to rain, so we don't know that at any minute, pop, something could happen and change it all around again.

MARGIE: I could certainly use something big happening before I settle in for the last run. *(Beat)* And what are you doing going back to St Louis? Who do you have there? There's nothing there.

ALMA: My mother.

MARGIE: She's in her grave.

ALMA: It's home.

MARGIE: Home's where you make your bed at night. Even a fool know that.

(Sound of a key in the lock. LOUIS enters.)

MARGIE: Well, well...look what the drifting sands blew in.

(Pause as all of them survey each other.)

LOUIS: If either of you ladies wants to catch Sinatra, I have an extra ticket.

MARGIE: I believe he's been canceled.

LOUIS: Rumor only. *(He nods to ALMA.)*

MARGIE: Rumor also has it you've met my friend, Alma Leroy.

LOUIS: I asked her to dance in the bar.

MARGIE: That's not the way I heard it.

LOUIS: *(To* MARGIE*)* Your eyes are all red.

MARGIE: Why did you come back upstairs?

LOUIS: Do you think it would be possible for us to be alone?

ALMA: I can leave if you like.

MARGIE: *(Hesitating, then)* She stays.

LOUIS: Okay. She stays. *(Silence. To* MARGIE*)* I thought I'd find you alone, that we'd try again.

MARGIE: Try what?

LOUIS: Maybe what you said before?

ALMA: She's *planning* to *adopt.*

MARGIE: Alma! Shush! *(To* LOUIS*)* You're drunk.

LOUIS: That's right.

MARGIE: *(To* ALMA*)* I was right. *(To* LOUIS*)* Too late. The time has now passed for my idea.

LOUIS: Wait a minute. I come back and offer to do it, and you make me feel like an idiot. You must think I'm a yo-yo. Come here, go away, come here, go away, don't get me pregnant, get me pregnant. What the hell do you want?

MARGIE: I don't know, but whatever it is, I know this—I can't seem to get it.

LOUIS: No one around here can seem to give it *or* get it. *(Beat)* I decided I owe you something.

MARGIE: Zero.

LOUIS: But you asked me.

MARGIE: I shouldn't have asked. Okay? I am humiliated that I asked. Now will you please get out of here!

LOUIS: Picture this anyway, you home making fudge. Kids would put some clip in your wings.

MARGIE: Well maybe I want some clip in my wings, something holding me down. *(Beat)* I'd like to know why you said you loved me on my birthday.

ALMA: *(To* MARGIE*)* I think you should let it go.

MARGIE: I will not let it go!

LOUIS: I don't intend to be put on trial.

MARGIE: I'm the one on trial here, Louis. I'm the one who said 'Yes, yes, anything, anytime, you call it, I'll buy it'. How come you said it?

LOUIS: People say things. I meant it at the moment. I looked forward to seeing you. You were the high point of my week. I must have done something for you too or you would have stopped seeing me.

ALMA: You bamboozled her.

LOUIS: *(To* ALMA*)* If I did, then she let me.

MARGIE: The man's right. *(Beat. To* LOUIS*)* Sonovabitch, you've got it all—little house with green hedges and darling children.

ALMA: Oh they're both top athletes.

MARGIE: All-American boys and he has a golden retriever too. That's what he says. And he's a good dancer. *(Mocking a tap dance)* And he makes a nice appearance, as my mother used to say.

LOUIS: *(Going over to* MARGIE *and starting to shake her)* You never said "No"! You never even said "Get out". I gave you....

MARGIE: A gold necklace! *(She rips off the gold necklace she is wearing, throwing it at* LOUIS. *It falls on the carpet.)*

LOUIS: Are you crazy? What are you doing? That was a present. I gave that to you. *(To* ALMA*)* She picked it out herself. *(To* MARGIE*)* You said "That's the one I want". *(To* ALMA*)* She picked it out from the store window.

MARGIE: I'm a whore. I could be bought. What else would you call selling yourself cheap? A good steak and a bottle of wine, a little fundamental lovemaking, some perfume for Christmas and a bauble for your birthday.

ALMA: Malcolm bought me this silk blouse to go home in.

MARGIE: Alma, shut up!

ALMA: *(To* LOUIS, *keeping right on going)* You know she was voted the prettiest girl in the class and the one with the most school spirit. Only one in history to win two awards. It's right in the yearbook.

LOUIS: I'm sure.

MARGIE: And still a prize winner, Alma! Still collecting blue ribbons. Very blue.

ALMA: Don't lose that spirit.

MARGIE: *(To* ALMA, *with* MARGIE's *back to the audience but facing* ALMA*)* And let you down, so you'd have to look at me? You bet! Here's the old spirit, Alma! The virtual Spirit of St Louis! *(She rips off her bathrobe and stands in her peach colored bra and bikinis.)* And all your dreaming about a place neither of us can get back to isn't going to change anything, not for all your wishing! You take a good look! *(Pause)* Getting a little old for a beauty queen here.

ALMA: You're not going to shock me. I've been halfway around the world and had to come back empty handed, so nothing shocks me.

LOUIS: I think all the neon out there flashing must have snapped everyone's brain.

MARGIE: In place.

ALMA: *(To* MARGIE, *struggling with her to put her robe back on)* You get dressed!

MARGIE: Don't stop me! I'm on a real roll! Catch me and you can have me where you want me. I've done it, he'll vouch for it, faster than it takes to give a memo. *(To* LOUIS*)* Oh, don't you want to keep doing it on the back seat of your Mercedes on our lunch break?

*(*ALMA *succeeds in finally just wrapping the robe around* MARGIE*)*

MARGIE: Don't you want to keep that status quo and take me around the world, one last time, with all the whitecaps breaking? *(*MARGIE *twirling, and then, exhausted)*

(Pause)

LOUIS: *(Silence)* Please, pick up the necklace.

(Silence. No one moves. LOUIS *starts to bend down.)*

MARGIE: *(Almost in tears)* Don't you dare. That's my necklace. It belongs to me.

LOUIS: You know what? This place is nuts. I'm going home.

ALMA: If I had one, I couldn't think of a better place to go.

(Note that MARGIE *is still wrapped in her bathrobe and remains so until the end of the scene.)*

LOUIS: *(Getting his suit bag out of the closet)* Alma, I hope your boy's okay and I salute you wherever you end up. *(He takes out his wallet, taking out three one hundred dollar bills and handing them to* ALMA*)* When you send it back, send it to my business address. Margie can give it to you.

*(*MARGIE *stares at the both of them.)*

LOUIS: And M G M's got all the time in the world so take your time.

ALMA: *(Taking the money, holding it)* Thank you, and I have to tell you the truth, Mr M G M...

MARGIE: Monaco—as in the principality of—

ALMA: *(Handing* LOUIS *back the money)* Monaco—I've decided on going back to San Francisco and banging down my sister's door, so I could hitch if I had to. *(Pause)* I'd have to walk backwards to get to St Louis. And I would never live in a condominium on Malibu anyway, not with all that water. I mean you gotta consider tidal waves and fires and earthquakes and such.

LOUIS: I only said "if". I never made a firm offer. (*To* MARGIE) And it's an English sheepdog, not a golden retriever. (*Hesitating, starting to touch* MARGIE)

MARGIE: Don't you touch me or I'll start to cry.

LOUIS: (*Pausing, then*) You're telling me about connection. I have to go back to what I chose because it's just not bad enough to leave, and I don't have the stomach to do anything else. (*Beat*) I could love you, Margie. Well maybe I did. I bet I did. (*He exits.*)

(*Pause*)

ALMA: The money was because I needed to get home and I asked him to lend it to me and I was going to pay it back.

MARGIE: I'll lend you what you need. If it didn't work out here, it won't work anywhere.... Louis was going to be a *major* filmmaker, I was going to be a movie star, discovered on Sunset Boulevard, and you were going to be....

ALMA: (*Saluting*) The Captain's wife. (*Pause*) You'll find someone better.

MARGIE: Yeah.

ALMA: And anyway, you got something. It may be the last thing you wanted, so it's the last thing you got, but you got yourself stuck with an old acquaintance here, and one thing people say about me... when you got me, I stick like glue.

(*A knock at the door.*)

MARGIE: We don't want it!

ALMA: No! No! It's probably room service.

FELIX: (*O S*) Room Service!

MARGIE: Coming!

(MARGIE *unlocks the door and* FELIX *enters, whistling, pushing the serving cart laden with breakfast. All the dishes are covered with silver domes.*)

MARGIE: It's the knight, come to save us.

FELIX: Rescue you from temptation. I told the kitchen I'd deliver this personally. I'm off duty with the news of the night! The French suite is free! (*He places the cart by the window and starts to set up, putting out three glasses for the champagne celebration. He has decided to get in on it.*)

MARGIE: Too bad, because we seem to have gotten a fix on what we have.

FELIX: Where's the Sheik of Araby?

(ALMA *lifts one of the covers on the tray, snitches a piece of bacon.*)

MARGIE: He left.

FELIX: *(As in a march)* He had a good girl but he left. I see. Hey, either of you interested in coming up to Lake Tahoe? Liza Minelli's singing there. She doesn't have her mother's face, but she can sure sing a song...

ALMA: Thank you.

MARGIE: *(Interrupting)* But we're planing on staying right here.

ALMA: Because here's where we are, if you know what I mean, so we might as well be.

(FELIX is opening the champagne.)

ALMA: *(Taking a bite of prune Danish)* Mmm...prunes. *(Offering a bite to* MARGIE*)* Hey, what ever happened to Sinatra?

FELIX: *(Pulling out the cork)* I am sorry to report that Francis Albert is not to be found anywhere and the money is being refunded. *(The cork pops.)*

ALMA: Hurray!

(FELIX pours the champagne into the three glasses.)

MARGIE: *(Bending down, picking the chain off the floor)* I think someone left this behind. *(Holding it out to* ALMA*)*

ALMA: No thanks.

MARGIE: *(Holding it out to* FELIX*)* I don't want it.

(FELIX hesitates, then picks it up.)

FELIX: *(Looking it over)* Twenty-four karat. Real gold.

MARGIE: Let's get out of here! Blow this town! *(Picking up the airline schedule still lying next to the phone)* Next flight out's at six A M. Come on! You call your sister, I'll get dressed, finish packing, we'll check out, call a cab, grab a cup of coffee on the road, drop you off at the Bus Station. Or, you want to fly? Tell the truth.

ALMA: *(Shaking her head "no")* I feel like riding for a long while, maybe running all the best times of my life across my head, like a movie...

MARGIE: *(Pushing the serving cart with the uneaten breakfast across the room and into the hallway as* ALMA *looks on longingly)* And tell that sister of yours, you're on your way and you're not taking "no" for an answer.

(MARGIE starts getting dressed and packed. ALMA *takes her address book out of her bag, also getting ready to go.)*

ALMA: What are you going to do about your job?

MARGIE: I don't know. I absolutely don't know. But I feel light-headed.

ALMA: Me too. Absolutely *light-headed. (Beat)* You know what? Turns out it's awfully hard to get a square meal around here.

*(It is still dark, but all the lights from outside illuminate the room; as they pack to leave, MARGIE begins humming...*You Are My Sunshine, *slowly, plaintively, then into the words, as ALMA joins in, in harmony. Perhaps it's a song they sang in Girl Scouts. ALMA picks up the pace at the end, as the lights fade, part words, part humming.)*

END OF PLAY

THE AGREEMENT

THE AGREEMENT was originally commissioned by National Public Radio for the Earplay series, directed by Tony Giordano, and broadcast on P B S in the U S, England, and Australia. The cast included Lou Jacobi, Marilyn Sokol, Lewis J Stadlen, Gail Godwin, Jill Eikenberry, and Michael Tucker. The first stage production was in 1985 at the Annenberg Center, Philadelphia Festival Theater for New Plays, Artistic Director, Carol Rocamora. THE AGREEMENT was directed by Julianne Boyd and published in *The Best Short Plays, 1986*.

THE AGREEMENT opened in New York in 1989 at the Manhattan Punch Line Theater. The cast and creative contributors were:

SYBIL . . . . .Susan Pellegrino
SIGMUND . . . . Richmond Hoxie
ALICE BAILEY . . . . Ilana Levine
LESTER OSTERNEYER . . . . Brian Keller
BORIS, JUDGE BELLOWS . . . . David Wasson
ALICIA . . . . Pat Nesbit

Director . . . . .Steve Kaplan
Lighting . . . . Brian MacDevitt
Set design . . . . .James Wolk

CHARACTERS

SYBIL MATCHETT
SIGMUND MATCHETT
ALICE BAILEY
LESTER OSTERMEYER
BORIS
ALICIA
JUDGE ALBERT BELLOWS
THE FRENCHMAN

Casting note: The same actor can play both the FRENCHMAN *and* JUDGE BELLOWS.

ACT ONE

Scene One

(Time: Sunday afternoon. Five P M. It is late June.)

(Place: The shabby and dismal room of a pension in the hills of Cap Antibes on the French Riviera, the Cote D'Azur. The room has two single beds. As the lights come up, SYBIL and SIGMUND enter, preceded by a young FRENCHMAN carrying two enormous pieces of luggage. SYBIL carries a small bouquet of pink tea roses. The two are breathing heavily from their climb to the sixth floor. The young FRENCHMAN stands with the luggage waiting for a direction from the two American tourists. SYBIL nods to a spot. The FRENCHMAN continues holding the luggage. SIGMUND points to the same spot. The FRENCHMAN puts the luggage down. The FRENCHMAN waits. SYBIL nods to SIGMUND indicating "the tip". SIGMUND digs in his pocket giving the FRENCHMAN a few francs. The FRENCHMAN nods to the flowers.)

FRENCHMAN: *Belle Fleures. Un vase pour les fleures?*

SYBIL: *Les fleures. Oui. (She hands the FRENCHMAN the flowers. To SIGMUND)* He's bringing us a vase. *(Turning back to the FRENCHMAN)* Merci. *(Then, pointing to SIGMUND)* Mon mari. *(Beat)* We are on our Honeyluna. *(Beat)* LUNA. *(Beat)* MOON.

FRENCHMAN: *(Smiling knowingly) Oui. Je comprends.*

SYBIL: *(To SIGMUND)* He understands.

FRENCHMAN: *Je reviens.*

SYBIL: *(To SIGMUND)* He will return.

(FRENCHMAN Exits.)

SIGMUND: You didn't have to tell him our business.

SYBIL: I'm sure he didn't understand a word I was saying.

SIGMUND: If you chat him up he'll expect a big tip.

SYBIL: He'll expect it anyway. This is the Cote D'Azur. *(Beat)* So what do you think of the room? I think it's sweet.

SIGMUND: It's fine. It's on a par with heaven. Heaven could not be any higher. *(Sitting on one of the beds)* The bed's saggy. Let's open the wine.

(Taking a bottle of the wine from their luggage. SYBIL exits into the bathroom.)

SIGMUND: I wish he would come so we can relax.

SYBIL: *(O S)* There are no glasses. And the bathroom's god-awful. Definitely bad. *Mal.*

(SIGMUND opens the wine. SYBIL enters. He offers her a drink. She shakes her head "No".)

SIGMUND: The bathroom has a toilet, I hope; not one of those crazy European holes in the ground.

SYBIL: It has a toilet, but the towels are threadbare and the tub's squalid. It has three small dead creatures in it.

SIGMUND: *(Taking off his shoes and shirt)* I thought you picked this place from the Guide Book.

SYBIL: I did. *(Getting the Guide Book out, reading)* " The Hotel La Guardiole occupies what once must have been a grand Chateau..."

SIGMUND: Too bad we missed it in its prime.

(He kisses the back of her neck as she sits on the sagging bed. She continues to read from the Guide Book.)

SYBIL: "'One of the loveliest hotels I have ever visited', said my friends Mike and Patty Torgeson."

SIGMUND: I thought we'd make love before dinner with the Mediterranean lapping jealously in the background.

SYBIL: *(Jumping up, still reading)* "One passes through an arched gateway into a courtyard with a lone palm rising." Do you remember any lone palm rising in the courtyard?

SIGMUND: *(Looking out the window)* No lone palm; but taste the wine. It's sensational.

(Handing SYBIL the bottle. She drinks from the bottle.)

SYBIL: Too sweet.

SIGMUND: Sauterne's sweet. It's supposed to be sweet. That's its nature. *(Pulling her down on the bed)*

SYBIL: I prefer dry.

SIGMUND: You should have said.

SYBIL: I thought you knew. *(Still reading from the book)* "The hotel stands in attractive and spacious gardens." *(She jumps up looking out the window)*

SIGMUND: Well I *didn't* know, but I do now. *(Continuing to drink)*

SYBIL: *(Reading on)* "A profusion of magnolias tumbles down the hillside..."

(SIGMUND gets up from the sagging bed, joins her by the window, caressing her. SYBIL cranes to see out the window.)

SYBIL: I don't see any magnolias.

SIGMUND: Maybe they're not in season.

(SYBIL *breaks away from* SIGMUND *getting a chair, standing on it while continuing to read the guide book.*)

SYBIL: Oh my God, Sigmund, will you listen to this!

SIGMUND: Will you stop popping up like a jumping jack! So the book's a pack of lies. So we picked it wrong. Who cares?

SYBIL: I care! I do! Look at this! (*Reading from the Guide*) "Looking out to the sea with stunning views of the village below." I do not see a speck of sea out there.

SIGMUND: Maybe it's the profusion of magnolias *not* in bloom obstructing our view.

SYBIL: (*Continuing to read*) "There is a delightful little terrace off the bedrooms where you can sun yourself or take afternoon tea." (*To* SIGMUND) Come here. Come here. Look out this window.

(*He does.*)

SYBIL: Do you or do you not see a terrace anywhere?

SIGMUND: If you don't like this room, we can go out. We can leave his tip, or give it to him later, or not at all. Or we can bolt the door and crawl under the covers and close our eyes.

SYBIL: I don't believe this. (*Lying down on the bed, reading*) "Sumptuous bathrooms, all with chandeliers, good firm beds..."

(*She bounces up and down on the bed continuing to bounce as the springs sag and groan.* SIGMUND *bounces up and down with her, not of his own volition.*)

SYBIL: "Each room is done in country antiques and cheerfully decorated with flowered wallpaper..." (*She looks about the room. The paint is peeling.*) "...In addition to fresh local flowers provided by the management." Something's cuckoo.

(SIGMUND *is trying to make love to her while* SYBIL *grows more and more obsessed with the guide book.*)

SYBIL: "Everything here is haute, the cuisine as well as the location."

SIGMUND: What does that mean? "Haute"?

SYBIL: High, I think. It implies "high". (*Reading*) "The owners are constantly engaged in improvements." Ha!

SIGMUND: (*Reading over her shoulder*) "Calvin Klein would never stay here but Ernest Hemingway would."

SYBIL: That's it! We're in the *wrong place*!

SIGMUND: So maybe we are.

SYBIL: Not maybe. Without question.

SIGMUND: The question is, do you care to make love, in the right or wrong place not withstanding?

SYBIL: I suppose you like being cheated. Well this hotel, frankly, depresses me. In fact, I'm getting into one of my Sunday afternoon angsts. I bet it's five o'clock. That's when it really gets bad. *(Checking her watch)* I knew it! I knew it! Five minutes to five. And this is only aggravating it. Here, for once, I could have slid right through the hour, looking out to the sea, sitting on the terrace, smelling the magnolias, drinking a great French Chardonnay.

SIGMUND: You pointed to this wine yourself. You pointed to this bottle in the window and said, "That's the one I want".

SYBIL: Until I had it. How was I supposed to know before I had it? But no need to be stuck, you know. *(Beat)* God, I hate this place! It's so tacky, so *degeulace... (Explaining)* Disgusting. So triste, so sad. It's absolutely making me blue.

SIGMUND: It's only a room.

SYBIL: But maybe we're in the wrong room. *(Beat)* I want another room. *(Touching him)* I just want everything to start out right, perfect, *tres jolie.*

(There is a knock at the door.)

SIGMUND: It's him. *(Calling out)* Yes? *Oui?*

FRENCHMAN: *(O S) Les fleures pour Madame.*

SIGMUND: Come in.

SYBIL: *Entrez.*

(The FRENCHMAN enters, handing the flowers, now in a crystal vase, to SYBIL. She smiles with approval, placing them on the windowsill.)

SYBIL: *(To FRENCHMAN)* We seem to have a problem here.

FRENCHMAN: *(Still smiling, always smiling)* Madame?

SYBIL: We are in the wrong place.

SIGMUND: *(Picking up the guide book)* According to this guide book... *(Opening it)* ...there are magnolias and a view of *la mer.*

FRENCHMAN: *(In strained English)* Have you seen the beach at Nice?

SYBIL: The problem is, this place is not as the guide book says.

SIGMUND: It appears to be misrepresented.

FRENCHMAN: The beach at Nice is nice. *(Pointing to the guide book)*

SYBIL: *(Waving the guide book, more frantic now)* It says in here, there is a terrace. Aha! Where's your terrace?

FRENCHMAN: *(Making movie reel movements with his hands)* Cannes...movies.

SIGMUND: My wife would like to change rooms.

SYBIL: It says in the guide book "Cheerfully decorated".

(There is no response.)

SIGMUND: *(Speaking slowly)* The room is bad. *(Beat)* Bad. *(Beat)* Bad room.

SYBIL: *Gauche.*

SIGMUND: *(Repeating her)* Gauche room.

SYBIL: It's just bad. *(To* SIGMUND*)* I forgot the word for bad. I'm so upset I forgot the word for "bad". *(Now pronouncing it as in "baa baa black sheep")* Baaad.

FRENCHMAN: *(Still strained)* The beach at Nice is nice. *(Straining for a different word)* Cheerful. Good.

SIGMUND: *(To* SYBIL*)* It's no use.

SYBIL: *(Angrily)* We are moving! I WANT TO MOVE!

FRENCHMAN: MOVIE! Cannes! *Ensolleile. (Making a signal for the sun in the sky, drawing it in the air)* The beach at Nice is nice. Always nice. And in Cannes, *mon dieu*, movies. Day and night. Night and day. Beaucoup movies. *(Acting out Gene Kelly in* Singing in the Rain, *actually singing, or Fred Astaire dancing, making believe he's holding onto Ginger Rogers humming "Dancing In the Dark")*

SIGMUND: *(Reaching into his pockets. Then to* SYBIL*)* Do you have any small francs?

SYBIL: *(Reaching into her purse)* What's ten francs?

SIGMUND: I don't know. Just give it to me. *(He takes the coins from her, hands it to the* FRENCHMAN.*)*

(The FRENCHMAN *smiles and stands there)*

FRENCHMAN: *Au revoir, Monsieur et Madame,* and you have given me as a gratuity approximately thirty cents.

SYBIL: *(To* SIGMUND*)* But what about changing the room?

SIGMUND: To hell with it. It's only one night. *(To* FRENCHMAN*)* Good night. *(To* SYBIL*)* If he doesn't leave I intend to close the door on his foot.

SYBIL: *(To* FRENCHMAN*)* *Bon soir, monsieur.*

(The FRENCHMAN *smiles and beats a quick exit.)*

SYBIL: I can stand anything else, but I hate filth. *(Taking a drink of wine from the bottle)*

SIGMUND: *(Caressing her)* Come lie down and make love to me.

(The sounds in the distance of violins tuning up.)

SYBIL: I'm not using the bed. Then we'll feel committed. You'll say, as long as we're using the bed we have to stay.

(Sounds of string quartet starting)

(Beat)

SYBIL: Do you hear that? *That's* the *music* they talked about in the guide book. I bet that's the music. Vivaldi, Concerto in G Minor. *(Grabbing the book, reading)* "At twilight a lovely string quartet serenades..." *(Looking out the window)* It's coming from over there, across the driveway, from the other hotel. I bet we're in the wrong hotel. I bet that's all it is. Please god that's what it is. We should go down and check. *You* should check.

SIGMUND: I can hear the music fine. And it sounds like Brahms.

SYBIL: No, I think it's Vivaldi. Shh...

(They listen intently.)

SYBIL: No. I think it's actually "La Vie en Rose."

SIGMUND: It could be Rodgers and Hart.

SYBIL: I think it's hard to tell. Are you going to check?

SIGMUND: It's starting to get dark. And what's the difference if there are flowers on the wall or not?

SYBIL: *(Looking out the window)* I know that's our hotel. We could call the desk. They could send someone up to carry the luggage. We didn't even use the towels. *(Standing on a chair, on tiptoe)* And I definitely see a terrace over there.

SIGMUND: I'm not giving him another franc.

SYBIL: We could carry our own luggage.

SIGMUND: Down six flights? Past the front desk? Across the driveway?

SYBIL: Sigmund...

SIGMUND: Yes, Sybil...

SYBIL: It's hard enough that it's Sunday, when I need to trick myself into thinking it's all okay, which I know it isn't, especially around five o'clock when I'm filled with this free-floating I-don't-know-where-it-came-from despair, when there's no turning back, when it gets icy blue before it turns black. *(Beat)* So can we move?

SIGMUND: Can we make love first?

SYBIL: That will only make matters worse. That makes me sad. I know it makes some people happy, but not me. Afterwards I always feel sad.

SIGMUND: You never said that before.

SYBIL: I thought you noticed how I'm always quiet afterwards.

SIGMUND: I thought it was contentment.

SYBIL: *(Shaking her head "no")* Terror.

(Lying down on the other single bed. They now lie on separate beds. The music drifts in.)

SIGMUND: *(Beat)* Is there something I'm doing wrong?

SYBIL: No. I feel this way with everyone. *(Beat)* But especially if I do it on a Sunday afternoon. Then it triggers my blue agita and feeds it and before I know it, it's escalated to such proportions.... *(Beat)* I find, for my own protection, I have to be very cautious on Sundays. *(Silence)* Do you want a piece of cheese? *(Opening her purse, taking out a small crushed napkin which holds a piece of runny brie, sticking to the napkin)* I saved it from breakfast. It's a lovely Brie.

SIGMUND: No thank you.

(SYBIL runs her finger through the melting cheese, puts her finger in her month, tastes the cheese, wraps it back in the napkin, puts it back in her purse. The music drifts farther away. It is getting darker.)

SYBIL: Should we unpack our luggage?

SIGMUND: I don't think so.

SYBIL: Should we move? What do you think?

SIGMUND: Yes. I think we should try another place.

(Lights fade)

(End of scene)

END OF ACT ONE

ACT TWO

Scene One

(Time: Early evening. Twelve years later.)

(Place: California. SYBIL's *apartment.* SYBIL *is with her date,* BORIS. *Her children are in an adjoining room.)*

SYBIL: *(Holding up a glass)* To rainy nights in California.

BORIS: *(Holding up his glass)* To rainy nights *(Pause)* and love in California. So, do you find it exciting writing for the movies?

SYBIL: Love it, and I've certainly never met a live stunt man before. What's the hardest stunt you ever did?

BORIS: The hardest stunt?

SYBIL: The hardest stunt—

BORIS: Well, I did this horror film and there's this forest fire....

SYBIL: *(Cutting him off and turning to the direction of the children)* Stop it! Stop it! Just eat your sushi! *(Back to* BORIS, *shrugging)* Kids. They like to shred it to aggravate me. Excuse me.

BORIS: No big deal. *(Continuing)* So, the entire world is enveloped by this forest fire.... *(Imitating the fire starting in spots over the world, jumping around)* Woo... Woo... Woo! Everything's burning! Poof! *(Pause)* Actually, just the parts that have forests.

SYBIL: Naturally.

BORIS: See, it starts out as this love story. What I'm talking about is...let me show you... *(Getting ready to jump)* This is *perfectly* safe. Don't worry.

SYBIL: No. I'm *perfectly* calm. *(To the children)* I hear you in there! If you're not going to eat it, stop throwing it! *(Back to* BORIS) This is really hard. *They're* jumping around, and you are...

BORIS: *SO,* it's this *love* story, and his girlfriend is down there in this forest burning, and he has to put her out...so he parachutes...like this— *(Parachuting, landing on the couch beside her, listing towards her)* Terrible film... But what do you think of my landing?

SYBIL: I'm impressed. *(To the children, without getting up)* Absolutely *not.* *(Back to* BORIS) In the winter, Sigmund—that's my ex—takes them to Florida to his mother's mobile home where they play Bingo all week at her Activity Center. This year he brought his girl friend, Auntie Bambi. The children said she combed her hair a lot. She also got bored with playing Bingo, so they went to Disneyworld where Sigmund and she wore matching Mickey Mouse shirts. *(To the children)* You are nearing the end of my rope!

BORIS: Here, let me help you. *(Getting up, yelling at the children)* Hey kids! Listen to your mother! HEY! HEY! *(Back to* SYBIL*)* So when do they go to sleep?

SYBIL: When they get tired.

BORIS: When is that usually?

SYBIL: It varies.

BORIS: I think it would be good if we could relax.

SYBIL: I am certainly trying.

BORIS: *(Breathing in on the word "Re" and out on "lax")* Re-Lax. Re-Lax.

*(*SYBIL *follows him, and they do the relaxation exercise in unison.)*

BORIS: Re-Lax. Re-Lax. Now when's your trial?

SYBIL: It's a pre-trial. Next week in New York. Thank you for asking.

BORIS: And how long have you been separated?

SYBIL: One year, eight months.

BORIS: Been dating?

SYBIL: I haven't slept with anybody yet if that's what you mean.

BORIS: How come?

SYBIL: Nobody's asked me.

BORIS: I'm asking you.

SYBIL: Boris, do you think I'll get the Russian samovar his Aunt Millie gave us, because it was *his* aunt, but she gave it to me, but I think I'm going to give him the pictures of the kids, seeing I have the real thing.

BORIS: *(Breathing in and out)* RE-LAX. RE-LAX. RE-LAX LAX LAX.

(End of scene)

Scene Two

(Lights fade down slowly on the above scene then up on the next scene.)

(Time: Early evening)

(Place: SIGMUND's *Manhattan apartment.* SIGMUND *and his date* ALICIA *are eating, almost finished with dinner.)*

ALICIA: Marvelous spaghetti *avec* pesto sauce, Sigmund.

SIGMUND: Thank you. It's my specialty. Don't bother twirling it around the fork. Just let it hang. So I have this house on the island which costs me a thousand dollars a month upkeep and it rains every damn weekend this summer.

ALICIA: What a shame. *Pauvre (Pronouncing the "e" as in eggs)* Sigmund.

SIGMUND: A thousand dollars a month shame.

ALICIA: I thought psychiatrists were rich, the urban population à la Woody Allen being tres neurotic.

SIGMUND: Not one's paying for the past *and* the present.

ALICIA: That sounds very psychological.

SIGMUND: It isn't. More scotch?

ALICIA: *Merci*, but no.

SIGMUND: An after dinner drink? Crème de cacao, crème de menthe, Manischevitz?

ALICIA: One scotch was fine. Beautiful view you have of Central Park.

SIGMUND: Thank you... It's curious, Alice....

ALICIA: *(Interrupting)* Alicia.

SIGMUND: Forgive me.

ALICIA: My name's Alicia.

SIGMUND: Alicia.

ALICIA: Thank you.

SIGMUND: You know, it's curious, Alicia...I forgot what I was going to say I got so concerned with the name. Oh yes, I was going to ask you if you were free next weekend.

ALICIA: I don't care for the Hamptons, thank you. They don't touch me.

SIGMUND: I see. They don't touch you.

ALICIA: And I think touching's important. How long were you married, Sigmund?

SIGMUND: Ten years. Well perhaps we can make other arrangements.

ALICIA: I've never been to the Virgin Islands.

SIGMUND: Neither have I. The Virgin Islands touch you?

ALICIA: Vastly.

SIGMUND: Vastly... Could you watch your ashes, Alicia. That's French country fabric on the sofa, eighteen ninety-nine a yard.

ALICIA: Have you ever been to Europe?

SIGMUND: When I was in the Army.

ALICIA: My former husband was in Korea.

SIGMUND: Good for him.

ALICIA: His name was Stanley, as in Marlon Brando in STREETCAR NAMED DESIRE.

SIGMUND: Good for Stanley.

ALICIA: He had a dark fear of intimacy, unlike Brando. So what do you think about the Virgin Islands?

SIGMUND: I can't. I have a pre-trial coming up.

ALICIA: Oh. I thought you were already divorced.

SIGMUND: Well, for all purposes, I am.

ALICIA: Well for my purposes, I wish you'd told me, because I only date *completely* free men, though I have to tell you, you make a terrific pesto sauce. *(Starting to leave)*

SIGMUND: I grate the cheese myself. Asiago. That's my secret. Not parmesan. Asiago—A-S-I-A-G-O.

ALICIA: Well I certainly admire that.

SIGMUND: But make sure it's fresh. Sometimes they say it's fresh when it's not fresh at all. Deceit is a dreadful thing in our society, you know.

ALICIA: And when you're free absolutely, *sans* doubt, I'd consider a return. I'll just catch a cab. Goodnight Sigmund.

(She exits as SIGMUND *muses, unaware, in a way, that's she's gone, more preoccupied.)*

SIGMUND: Unfortunately, she took the Cuisinart, because that's the way to really pulverize cheese, but I'm demanding it back because I know she never uses it because she never figured out which parts go where on anything. Sybil's very unmechanical. I also want the little Mexican god we bought in Guadalajara because she insisted it looked like me. it's actually a rendering of the god, Quetzelcoatal. She called him "Quetzal". It rhymes with "pretzel". Do you know she was late for our wedding ceremony? We had to pay overtime for the hall.

(End of scene)

Scene Three

VOICE: *(Over loud speaker system)* Court of the Southern District of New York, Probate Division, Judge Albert Bellows presiding. First case, Farrow versus Farrow.

(Time: Morning, one week later.)

(Place: Manhattan courthouse corridor)

(We see ALICE BAILY. SYBIL enters, breathless, somewhat disheveled.)

SYBIL: Am I late? The plane was late. There were seagulls on the runway.

ALICE: Relax. We're fifth in line. We'll go over some things here in the corridor.

SYBIL: I'm sorry, Mrs Bailey. I'm always late. I was late for my own honeymoon. We went to the Cote D'Azur.

ALICE: *(Interrupting SYBIL)* Beautiful day for a divorce, Mrs Matchett. We'll probably be here all day. They're booked solid.

SYBIL: It drove Sigmund crazy, my being late, because he's so compulsive. He said it was part of my complicated neurosis.

ALICE: Just take a seat on the bench until we're called. And Judge Bellows may not call you and Dr Matchett in on a pre-trial. He dislikes being involved with the inevitable emotions of the adversaries.

SYBIL: What does that mean?

ALICE: The judge gets the information from the lawyers, and then we lawyers translate the information to you and you say yes or no. *(Pause)* It eliminates the middle man.

SYBIL: Us.

ALICE: Precisely. You wait outside while the lawyers talk to the Judge. Now what were the taxes on your house in California last year?

SYBIL: Well I should think it would help the Judge if he could see the real people.

ALICE: The taxes...

SYBIL: They're somewhere here... *(Dumping out the contents of her bag)* In the bottom of my pocketbook. The children gave me this candy bar *(Pulling out a melted candy bar and credit cards)* as a goodbye present at the airport, but it's melting all over my credit cards.

ALICE: This is no joking matter, Mrs Matchett. I need the tax figures.

SYBIL: I think I'm not hearing you on purpose because I'm scared.

ALICE: *(Sharply)* Well no one would know it. You look awfully gorgeous.

SYBIL: Thank you. It's an Oscar De La Renta. He does this dot thing.

ALICE: You might have done better to dress down.

SYBIL: You mean dress a little poor.

ALICE: Precisely. It would have been in better taste.

SYBIL: What a dilemma, because I wanted to feel good too. *(Still searching)* Here it is... *(Taking out the paper)* Two sixty-four Mullholland Drive, four thousand six hundred dollars.

ALICE: Good.

SYBIL: Why is it good?

ALICE: It's high. Your expenses are high. That's good. We'll have a better case against the enemy.

SYBIL: The enemy...

ALICE: Regarding medical and dental, are your children currently undergoing orthodonture or do you plan orthodonture?

SYBIL: Are you kidding? Have you looked in their father's mouth?

ALICE: Truthfully, I'm thorough, but no.

SYBIL: Awful. The children have dreadful malocclusions, and Sigmund comes from a long line of malocclusers, so it's his side that they get the bad bite from, so I feel he ought to be responsible.

ALICE: We're not talking about right or wrong here, Mrs Matchett.

SYBIL: *(Breaking in)* But their bite...

ALICE: I can only promise a good fight, not justice.

SYBIL: God!

ALICE: There's no agreement made in heaven. A good agreement is only what's good for both parties.

SYBIL: That's very philosophical, Mrs Bailey.

ALICE: Thank you. And your husband and Mr Ostermeyer, his counsel, are late.

SYBIL: And Sigmund has awful vision. I think we ought to put something in the agreement about future opthomological care. When you think about the things that *could* happen in the future because *he* was their father.

ALICE: Just wait until you meet your husband's counselor, Lester Ostermeyer, if you think you've got trouble now. And I thought your husband was always on time.

SYBIL: He might have a queasy stomach. Sigmund's stomach turns over when he's nervous. I used to make him hot water and lemon juice.

ALICE: Dr Matchett is also asking for his exercycle, Mrs Matchett.

SYBIL: That's ridiculous. He hasn't used it in ten years. He hasn't used a lot of things in ten years.

ALICE: Divorce wroughts many changes.

SYBIL: Someone said he gained twenty pounds after I left.

ALICE: He looked quite trim when he came to my office.

SYBIL: Was he wearing a vest? I bet he was wearing a vest.

ALICE: He could have been. Yes.

SYBIL: Well watch out. He hides everything under vests. Do you think he's attractive?

ALICE: Are you kidding? Those blue eyes? That head of hair?

SYBIL: Head of hair?! He must have had a transplant. Was he wearing glasses?

ALICE: Not that I recall. What were the utilities last year, Mrs Matchett?

SYBIL: I knew it! Contact lenses. He probably had plastic surgery too. I may not even recognize him. He's a very vain person, Mrs Bailey. I think the Judge ought to know this. I had to fight him for the mirror every morning. Did you notice his nervous tick?

ALICE: Quite frankly, I found his eyes distracting, so I tried not to look into them.

SYBIL: No. It's in his left knee. It goes off at three minutes intervals. It developed shortly after we married. All of a sudden the knee just pops out like a cuckoo clock.

ALICE: I wouldn't mention that.

SYBIL: Mention *what*?

ALICE: That it happened *after* you were married. Discretion is the name of the game here.

SYBIL: Well I'm certainly not responsible, Mrs Bailey, for everything that happened *after* we were married.

ALICE: Potentially.

SYBIL: God!

ALICE: Dr Matchett also mentions a sheepdog.

SYBIL: Snowflake.

ALICE: He just stated "The Sheepdog".

SYBIL: He slept with it.

ALICE: Every night?

SYBIL: Uh huh.

ALICE: Let me get this down. *(Writing)* Slept with the sheepdog... Were you in the same bed with Dr Matchett and his sheepdog?

SYBIL: *(Adamant)* Our sex life was very hot. I tested out of the range listed in *Vanity Fair's* quiz.

ALICE: I'm trying to make a case for you here, Mrs Matchett. That is the name of the game. Now you understand this could qualify as sexual deprival and/or depravity. What exactly did Dr Matchett do with this dog, Mrs Matchett?

SYBIL: I bought Snowflake in the stuffed animal department of F A O Schwartz. Sigmund kept it on top of the bed as you would a toss pillow.

ALICE: This *is* a bummer.

O S VOICE: Next case... Connely versus Connely.

ALICE: *(Reading from her list)* The Sam Francis painting of Point Bobo at Sunset.

SYBIL: Point *Lobo*, Mrs Bailey, *Lo-Bo*.

ALICE: *(Reading)* Also asking for the Cuisinart, the sailboat...

SYBIL: *(Surprised)* What?

ALICE: Well he can *ask* for anything he wants.

SYBIL: Whose side are you on, Mrs Bailey?

ALICE: It doesn't mean he's going to get it.

(LESTER OSTERMEYER and SIGMUND *enter, deeply involved in discussion, looking at papers.)*

ALICE: There he is! That's Mr Ostermeyer, his counselor, the man with him. Don't worry, Mrs Matchett. You know what they say about me. My knife goes in so quietly you never see the blood.

SYBIL: Sigmund looks terrible. I hate the hair.

ALICE: Just be charming to him. A little honey never hurts.

SYBIL: His back is bothering him. I can tell by the way he's walking crooked.

ALICE: Just be calm and don't give them any information. And be advised that your husband's counselor, Lester Ostermeyer, is going through a divorce himself.

SYBIL: *(Whispering as the men come nearer)* Is that good?

ALICE: Oh no. That's bad. Very bad.

SYBIL: *(Repeating)* Very bad.

ALICE: He hates all women now. His wife ran away with her secretary.

(Fifteen minutes later. Lights fade out then up in corridor outside courtroom.)

ALICE: My client, Sybil Matchett, is requesting ownership of the sailboat, *The Sybil.*

SIGMUND: Sybil can't even sail.

ALICE: She could learn to sail, Dr Matchett.

SYBIL: I could learn to sail.

LESTER: That boat gives *my* client inordinate seasonal pleasure.

ALICE: I'm sure. I understand he does a lot of "springy" entertaining on board.

LESTER: He's too busy working so he can make his payments to Mrs Matchett.

ALICE: Not too busy working to take a vacation in Florida last year.

LESTER: To visit his aged mother.

SIGMUND: My aged mother.

SYBIL: My foot, Sigmund.

ALICE: And snuck a trip to Disneyworld, four days at the folksy Dutch Inn, one hundred and forty dollars a night.

SIGMUND: I object! That was for two rooms and I had the children.

SYBIL: Auntie Bambi slept in *his* room I'll bet.

LESTER: My client has every right to participate in social contact with the opposite sex.

ALICE: Your client took some bunny on a trip.

LESTER: Bambi LeClair is a social worker.

ALICE: Oh I'll bet she is with a name like that. *(Turning back to the case)* My client, as noted in Document one hundred and fifty-nine *(Reading)* is asking for the following: the property on West 83rd Street in Manhattan and the furnishing thereof, the summer property on Long Island and the furnishings thereof, the piece of land purchased jointly, and let me add hastily, in Spanish Lakes, located in the deserted desert of Arizona.

SIGMUND: Oh boy, another tall tale.

LESTER: May I understand, Mrs Bailey, the only thing *not* under contest is the children, custody awarded to *your* client.

SYBIL: *(To* ALICE*)* Is that a win or a lose?

ALICE: Please refrain from any comments, Mrs Matchett.

LESTER: That's right, Mrs Matchett, a little restraint here and on your Master Charge.

SIGMUND: I'll drink to that.

ALICE: You're out of order, Mr Ostermeyer, and your client.

LESTER: You're never going to get what you're asking for, Mrs Bailey. You must think I'm representing Rockefeller here.

ALICE: You're going to be weeping in your scotch, Lester Ostermeyer. I'm warning you.

LESTER: Blow it out your bloomers, Alice. Where are we on the list?

ALICE: Two more cases before us, and I doubt we'll come to any agreeable agreement here today since your client is making outrageous demands.

LESTER: Just wait until we get into her artsy-craftsy life in sunny California.

ALICE: Who *is* Bambi LeClair?

LESTER: We understand Sybil Matchett associates with women—*a lot!*

ALICE: Sybil Matchett is a model mother.

LESTER: But can she bake an apple pie?

SYBIL: Yes I can.

SIGMUND: Yes she can! She certainly can. I was married to her so I know.

SYBIL: I wish this was over, Sigmund.

SIGMUND: It takes a lot of digging to bury the past, Sybil.

O S VOICE: Next case, Wolf versus Wolf.

(Lights fade. Spot on SIGMUND D S)

SIGMUND: The day I asked her to marry me, in Truro, Massachusetts, which means "truth" and is on Cape Cod, was sunny. We were invited guests for that weekend. It was August, 1969, and the nights were already beginning to get cold. Sharon Tate and her friends had just been murdered, John Kennedy had been dead for six years and Robert Kennedy for one. That weekend in Truro, we rowed across the lake in a brown wooden boat to a beach where the sign said "Private, No Trespassing". It was hazy and the fog was beginning to roll in. "I'll love you forever" I said. The name of the boat was "Someday".

(Lights down on SIGMUND and up on SYBIL D S.)

SYBIL: If you want to know why I married him, the beginning of everything, I would have to tell you pea soup. He was a senior at Amherst and had an apartment over Russo's Liquors. He invited me for the weekend. I was a junior at Wellesley and it cost eleven dollars round trip on the Peter Pan Bus Lines. I arrived in a well underway snowstorm and we made pea soup together, he peeling the carrots, me adding the peas. We ate it sitting at a four legged maple table by the window, with French bread, which we dipped. Outside the snow was falling on the spruce trees in the public park. It was green and white outside and in. Afterwards we made love, of course.

(Lights fade, then up again on courtroom corridor.)

SYBIL: It was a B minus over C plus marriage which was hard to leave.

SIGMUND: We had our differences.

SYBIL: Which are nobody's business.

ALICE: The specifics would be helpful, Matchetts.

LESTER: I don't know how you expect us to fight this case without ammunition.

SIGMUND: God, all we want is an agreement.

ALICE: Cut the baloney, Doctor. You preyed on this woman, demanding favors, refusing coffee of the instant type, laughing at her large buttocks.

SYBIL: Mrs Bailey, please!

SIGMUND: Thank you.

SYBIL: No dirty linen.

SIGMUND: We'll wash our own.

SYBIL: And I don't have large buttocks.

SIGMUND: No she doesn't.

SYBIL: Thanks, darling.

SIGMUND: The pleasure's mine.

LESTER: *(Officially)* The marriage has irretrievably broken down.

ALICE: *(Officially)* Non-aligned chemistry.

SIGMUND: We simply grew in different ways.

SYBIL: Like a cactus and a violet.

ALICE: My client is also demanding the bicycle built for two.

LESTER: My client is not shipping a tandem bike cross-country.

ALICE: Then *my* client will forget to send *your* client the slides. They'll slip her mind.

LESTER: Which you must admit is already pretty slippery. Things just fall in and out of it.

SYBIL: Wait a minute. You're talking about me. He's talking about me, Sigmund. He's insulting me.

SIGMUND: All's fair.

SYBIL: What's fair? How you came in the middle of the night and absconded with our entire set of classical C Ds?

SIGMUND: It was three o'clock on a Sunday afternoon, I'd just flown in from New York, I was visiting my two children, and she said "take anything, I don't care".

ALICE: *(To* SYBIL*)* My God, is this true? You said "take anything"?

SYBIL: I didn't care at the moment.

ALICE: My client was crazed from temporal disappointment.

SIGMUND: Sybil was never crazed. She is a very rational woman.

SYBIL: Thank you, Sigmund.

SIGMUND: You're welcome, and she lives in California, so what would she want with classical music?

SYBIL: Right. We're too busy tossing about on the tennis courts.

LESTER: I suggest they split the collection—she'll take the Bach through Liszt, he'll get Mozart through Wagner.

ALICE: I object. Then my client loses Rachmaninoff and Tchaikovsky.

SYBIL: And I love the Russians.

SIGMUND: God, you can't have the world!

SYBIL: He has all our books, a green leather bound version of *The Rubaiyat of Omar Khayyam* which he inscribed "To my sweetheart, and the night shall be filled with music", boxed in his mother's basement.

SIGMUND: Safe in Mamaroneck.

SYBIL: Molding away. How is your mother?

SIGMUND: She had a heart attack and is in a recuperative home.

SYBIL: A home! My God! Couldn't your sister Helen take her in?

ALICE: Keep to the necessary confusions, please. We are about to be called. State your requests clearly.

LESTER: In tangible terms.

SYBIL: Twenty-five.

SIGMUND: Thousand?!

SYBIL: Until there's a change in my situation.

SIGMUND: Like what?

SYBIL: Success.

SIGMUND: I heartily wish it for you.

SYBIL: From the depths of your pocketbook, I'm sure.

ALICE: Let me remind you visitation rights have to be settled.

SIGMUND: I want the children every summer.

SYBIL: Fine.

SIGMUND: For two weeks.

LESTER: In any state my client wishes.

ALICE: *(To* SYBIL*)* You don't have to agree to any location lock-in.

SYBIL: Then I won't. I have no idea what state I'll be in.

ALICE: All my client wants is a sense of security. She wants Dr Matchett to put his assets *not* in wine or women, but in his family. Trust Funds.

SIGMUND: Security comes from within.

LESTER: A-men.

SYBIL: Sigmund always talks like a psychiatrist when it comes to money because he's cheap.

SIGMUND: If Sybil were to lay all the baubles I've given her, they would stretch across the Lobby of the Plaza Hotel where I took her on her wedding night.

SYBIL: *Our* wedding night, Sigmund, *OUR*.

SIGMUND: The next day we were leaving for the French Riviera.

(Lights fade out. Spot up on SIGMUND *D S.)*

SIGMUND: I wanted everything to be perfect. I was very much in love with her. I ordered the bridal suite. There were mirrors on the ceiling.

(Lights down on SIGMUND, *up on* SYBIL *D S.)*

SYBIL: We brought our own candles. Hand dipped. I was nervous. The ceiling had mirrors. I couldn't look. I was very young and Sigmund was the world.

(Lights fade, then up on courtroom corridor.)

SIGMUND: She kept telling me she felt sick, at ninety-five dollars a night, in those days.

SYBIL: I kept telling him I felt nauseous.

SIGMUND: I told her I loved her.

SYBIL: I told him I thought I was going to throw up.

(Lights fade, up on SIGMUND.*)*

SIGMUND: We had dreams, trips we wanted to make, children we wanted to have, how we were special, lucky....

(Lights fade, up on SYBIL*)*

SYBIL: Sigmund was wise about things no one else was wise about and he knew all the verses to "My Darling Clementine" which he sang to me lying in bed at the Plaza Hotel. He sang them off key, which was the only was he

knew, lying there, the city sounds outside us.... (*Singing a little off key*)
" You are lost and gone forever
La dee da da da da dee"

(Lights fade and up on SIGMUND.*)*

SIGMUND: We read "The Prophet" aloud to each other by candlelight, in the beginning. Her hair was brown and silky and we promised never to take anything for granted, like our luck. But it turned out that luck had nothing to do with anything.

(Lights fade back up on courtroom corridor.)

SIGMUND: Mrs Matchett threw up on our wedding night.

ALICE: I don't find that evidence of anything to my client's detriment.

SYBIL: Well I was much better in the morning.

SIGMUND: The next morning I had breakfast sent up.

SYBIL: It came on a silver tray with a red rose.

SIGMUND: Which was wilting. I ordered fresh strawberries out of season. It was December.

SYBIL: It was snowing and carriages were lined up in the park.

SIGMUND: She said she wanted to go out for a ride in the snow, so we did.

SYBIL: Three times around the park. I said "Let's ride until the sun comes out".

SIGMUND: Only it never did.

SYBIL: So we went back to the room.

SIGMUND: Back to bed.

SYBIL: They had white satin sheets.

SIGMUND: And she threw up again.

SYBIL: Well it turned out I had the flu. Our honeymoon was no picnic.

ALICE: My client requests full medical and dental.

SIGMUND: Only I refuse to pay for another gum job. She already had one gum job, and if she doesn't floss, it's not my fault.

SYBIL: I stimulate with toothpicks every night.

LESTER: My client does, however, deed to his soon to be former wife, their jointly owned cemetery plots.

ALICE: My client accepts.

SYBIL: I do not! They don't even have a view. He bought them in the most crowded part of the cemetery, way in the back, because it's cheaper.

SIGMUND: That's my Sybil! Always has to be a star!

SYBIL: I'm *not* your Sybil anymore, and I've decided to be cremated. Everyone in California is cremated.

SIGMUND: That's the American way. Out of sight, out of mind.

LESTER: Let's just divide the plots evenly then.

SYBIL: I'm not being buried next to him.

ALICE: Then I'll take them. I have no need for front and center.

LESTER: Thank you, Mrs Bailey.

ALICE: Let's get underway then.

LESTER: To proceed.

LESTER: I want the Cuisinart returned.

SYBIL: The Cuisinart's broken.

SIGMUND: *(To SYBIL)* What did you do to it?

SYBIL: I don't think an avocado should harm a Cuisinart.

SIGMUND: No. Not unless you put it in with the pit. Where's the warrantee?

SYBIL: I lost it.

SIGMUND: WHAT?

ALICE: My client says she has lost it.

SIGMUND: My lawyer can hear what your client, who is my wife, says. I'm telling you, Lester, she's highly irresponsible. I don't know, letting the children go off with her.

SYBIL: *(Sarcastically)* Then take them, please Sigmund.

SIGMUND: *(To SYBIL)* I wouldn't want to hog all the assets. On the other hand, candidly, Sybil is a highly eccentric and bizarre personality. And an oral compulsive. Twinkies by the ton, undercover.

SYBIL: He is a highly rigid and obsessive person, an anal compulsive.

ALICE: Sounds like the perfect match.

SYBIL: Mrs Bailey, whose side are you on?

LESTER: How was your wife's eccentricity manifested, Dr Matchett?

SIGMUND: When driving she would only make *left* turns, refused to make rights.

SYBIL: I'm afraid of rights. He knows that.

SIGMUND: We would just drive around and around and...it also severely limited our sexual activity.

ALICE: I should also mention, then, that Dr Matchett, a highly revered psychiatrist, wears his bunny slippers to bed because he says they make him feel more secure. I mean he already has his stuffed sheepdog.

SIGMUND: I have poor circulation.

SYBIL: The bunny slippers have little blue furry ears and button eyes.

SIGMUND: Why don't I tell them how you sleep with your mouth open.

SYBIL: I have a deviated septum.

SIGMUND: Which causes a loud locomotive-like sound.

LESTER: In other words, Mrs Matchett snores. (To SYBIL) And I also understand you have a hot tub in your backyard. Who's been in your tub lately, Mrs Matchett? And how hot is it? Rub a dub dub, three men in a tub.

ALICE: I consider these innuendoes highly unprofessional.

LESTER: Come on, Alice, you're defending a hot chick here. Admit it.

SYBIL: I am not a hot chick.

SIGMUND: My wife is definitely not a hot chick.

SYBIL: Thank you, Sigmund.

LESTER: (To SIGMUND) I'm your lawyer and I'm simply trying to establish here that Mrs Matchett is a rotten mother and that you owe her nothing.

SIGMUND: But that's not true. Sybil is a very dedicated mother...scouts, cake sales, bedtime stories, the whole bit, four stars.

LESTER: Oh terrific, Dr Matchett, that's terrific. Keep it up!

ALICE: In my opinion, Mrs Matchett is one of the most beautiful women to ever come across my desk.

LESTER: (To ALICE) Well no one asked for your opinion.

ALICE: My colleague here seems to think my opinion is worthless.

LESTER: You women think you're the only ones in the world who ever poached an egg, prepared a report, and looked gorgeous—all on the same day.

ALICE: I think you should be disqualified for that sexist statement.

LESTER: I'm not quitting now, just when the juices are beginning to run.

SYBIL: Well don't count on my juice, Ostermeyer.

SIGMUND: Mrs Matchett and I came for an agreement, not a carnage. I want this stopped, Lester.

LESTER: You want a case or not, Dr Matchett?

SIGMUND: You're harassing my wife.

ALICE: You are, Lester. You are in contempt of the court and my client.

LESTER: *(To* ALICE*)* You haven't got a case and you know it. Sybil Matchett's crazy, a highly eccentric personality, classified according to the American Psychiatric Association under file #509, "Bizzarity as a Classical Disorder".

ALICE: Come on, Lester, everyone knows all psychiatrists are nuts, including your client.

LESTER: My client is paying me a hundred twenty-five dollars an hour to determine exactly who the crazy one is.

SIGMUND: Don't remind me.

SYBIL: *(To* SIGMUND*)* You're shaking.

SIGMUND: It's my stomach.

SYBIL: No, I think it's your knee.

O S VOICE: Next case...Matchett versus Matchett. *(Loud Speaker)*

SYBIL: That's us!

O S VOICE: Counselors only.

SIGMUND: What does that mean?

LESTER: The Judge is going to try and mediate without you and Mrs Matchett there.

ALICE: Around the corner there's a small café. You two go off and have a drink.

LESTER: Have yourselves a Bloody Mary.

ALICE: We'll deal with the Judge. We know what you're fighting for. And on the boat, the *Sybil,* Sybil, how much is it worth roughly?

SYBIL: Why don't you let Sigmund have it. To tell you the truth, I don't know the bow *(pronounced "o")* from the rudder.

LESTER: Aha! She admits it!

ALICE: She admits nothing. Come on, Lester. The Judge is waiting. This is war!

(Lights fade out)

(End of scene)

Scene Four

(Time: One half hour later)

*(Place: "A Small Café" * SYBIL *and* SIGMUND *are seated at a table. Jazz plays. They have a drink and a sandwich.)*

SIGMUND: I thought you don't drink.

SYBIL: I do now. I like your contacts.

SIGMUND: I got a transplant.

SYBIL: I'm working on a word processor.

SIGMUND: I've learned to cook on a wok.

SYBIL: I joined a spa.

SIGMUND: I'm taking a Great Books Course at Columbia. We read Plato last week.

SYBIL: I finally read *The Brothers Karamazov*.

SIGMUND: I miss the kids.

SYBIL: They miss you. Julie had the lead in the Thanksgiving play. She was Pocahontas.

SIGMUND: I know. She wrote me.

SYBIL: I have the pictures. (*Taking them out*)

SIGMUND: (*Peeking a look*) She's pretty. She has your mouth. (*Then abruptly*) Beautiful day. Warm. Sunny.

SYBIL: Feels like home, breathing in all those good Manhattan fumes. I miss New York.

SIGMUND: More happens on any given day in a closet in New York than in an entire city anyplace in America.

SYBIL: We don't have good jazz in L A. Nobody's blue, I guess. (*Offering him a cigarette*) Cigarette?

SIGMUND: Thanks. I gave up smoking too.

(SYBIL *lights up*)

SYBIL: Too.

SIGMUND: Too. You didn't notice I wasn't smoking in the courthouse this morning?

SYBIL: I guess you weren't.

SIGMUND: No I wasn't.

SYBIL: Well I'm impressed.

SIGMUND: Well you should be.

SYBIL: Please don't tell me what I should be.

SIGMUND: It was a long process. I was hypnotized five times. I'm in a trance right now. (*Pause*) I've decided not to ask for the other night table. I don't want to break up a matched pair.

SYBIL: Thank you.

SIGMUND: And I know you'll be sad to learn that my Uncle Al died last month. Zap. Just like that. I think he died of loneliness with Aunt Celia gone.

SYBIL: Gone?! Sigmund!

SIGMUND: I mean you go to the other side of the continent, you expect life to stop.

SYBIL: You could have called me.

SIGMUND: We *are* getting divorced.

SYBIL: Well I still like your family. It was you I didn't like. *(Pause)* I don't know what to do with our wedding pictures.

SIGMUND: I don't know what to do with your father's pocket watch your mother gave me... Better head back for the Courthouse. Maybe they've come to a decision. *(Calling)* Waitress!

SYBIL *(Interior)* It was the thickest pea soup this side of Austria and we ate it sitting at a four legged maple table by the window.

SIGMUND: Before we go back, I have something to tell you. You were a winning wife. You're funny, you're warm, I love your face and your meatless moussaka and the shape of your mouth which is bow shaped which is what the kid's is, and I don't know what happened. I just got crazy. I don't know what it is I wanted...I still don't.

SYBIL: You wanted a divorce. You said you didn't love me anymore.

SIGMUND: I hate going to sleep by myself at night and waking up all alone on Sundays which are terrible. Where's the waitress? *(Calling)* Miss! *(Pause, then abruptly)* How's your social life?

SYBIL: Dating a lot. How's yours?

SIGMUND: Dating a lot. *(Pause)* It stinks. That's correct. I date a lot. I have dated twenty-two women in the past year and I have noted a certain pattern; they work out, they drink white wine, and make Caesar salads on request. Oh the Caesar salads I've conquered, the millions of croutons and blue cheese.

SYBIL: Well no one can do eggs once over light the way you can.

SIGMUND: Last winter I went up to Bromley. I rode past our house. They let the maples get too high; they block the whole view of the mountains.

SYBIL: That was a good house.

SIGMUND: We made love that time in front of the fireplace after the kids went to sleep.

SYBIL: Stop. You're making me crazy. It's history.

SIGMUND: It's *our* history *(Pause)* Why did you stop coming to bed when I went up to bed? Staying downstairs...?

SYBIL: I was afraid you wouldn't ask me if I wanted to.

SIGMUND: But if you didn't come, how could I ask you?

(Lights fade. End of scene)

Scene Four

(Time: Same time)

(Place: Lights fade up on JUDGE BELLOWS's chambers. JUDGE, ALICE, and LESTER)

JUDGE: They all want it all but you can't give them what there isn't nor can you divide what's indivisible.

ALICE: You can't fight over the contents of an empty pocketbook, your honor.

LESTER: And you can't argue over the water in an empty well, sir.

JUDGE: Precisely.

LESTER: What, then, is your proposal on their periodontal care, Judge Bellows?

JUDGE: Brush better. Brush three times a day. Your gums are your own responsibility.

ALICE: This agreement appears in order, Judge. We'll present it to the Matchetts.

JUDGE: If they can't agree, tell them they'll have to come to court, but there's a four-year back-up, by which time no one will remember *or* care anymore about who gets the pet cat.

ALICE: Dog.

JUDGE: See, I've already forgotten. And without passion there are no victories. Good Afternoon, counselors. Pleasure to see the A Team together again, stopping at nothing. Oh and Lester, how's *yours* going?

LESTER: Fine thank you, sir. Very civilized. Since we can't come to any decisions yet, my wife is occupying the bottom floor of our home and I have the top. She got the kitchen so I'm simply taking all my meals out...but I got the bathroom, which seemed more essential.

JUDGE: I'd say so. Good luck with the Matchetts. Tell them I said compromise is the cornerstone of conciliation.

ALICE: You bet, your honor.   •

JUDGE: And Alice, how's the *Big Romance* going? Any chance of wedding bells?

ALICE: Nothing ringing this year, your honor. Always hoping.

JUDGE: Just keep your sunny side up—NEXT!

(Lights fade out.)

(End of scene)

Scene Six

(Time: Immediately following)

(Place: Courthouse corridor)

ALICE: There they are! *(Calling)* Dr and Mrs Matchett! Here we are! *(To* LESTER*)* They're a handsome couple, don't you think? Wholesome.

LESTER: We're divorcing them, Alice.

SYBIL: What did Judge Bellows say?

LESTER: You'd better agree today. If you hesitate, you'll forget why you're getting a divorce in the first place.

ALICE: We may be coming very close to an agreement here.

(Both lawyers write quickly during next scene on legal pads.)

LESTER: *(Rapidly)* To him, all statuary.

ALICE: *(Rapidly)* To her, all paintings.

LESTER: To him, all loose lamps.

ALICE: To her, all fixed lighting.

LESTER: To each, all gifts from the other's family.

ALICE: As in *his* Aunt Millie's samovar to *her.*

LESTER: And *her* mother's silver service to *him,* as *he* polished it.

ALICE: As the party of either side claims it was their charms which wooed the other's family, in contrast to their own.

LESTER: Wherein the adage familiarity breeds contempt.

SIGMUND: *(To* SYBIL*)* I thought you might come out to California for Christmas.

SYBIL: Last Christmas Day the kids and I went to a movie with another divorced family. It was supposed to be a comedy, but it was very sad and we all cried.

LESTER: I think we're getting close on this agreement.

SIGMUND: I think you took my bathrobe when you left, Sybil.

ALICE: Before we tie things up here, Dr and Mrs Matchett, we'll have to renegotiate the life insurance.

SIGMUND: My green velour robe.

SYBIL: I wear it around.

SIGMUND: It's a *real* robe.

SYBIL: Yes it is.

LESTER: *(To* SIGMUND*)* If you let her keep the lithograph of Rodin's "The Screaming Woman" and the Cuisinart.

ALICE: *(Breaking in)* Which is broken. *(To* SYBIL *who is staring into* SIGMUND's *eyes)* Mrs Matchett, pay attention here. Your whole future's at stake.

SYBIL: Hardly over a Cuisinart.

ALICE: We are working our way *up*, if you please. Now his lawyer's carved out a three year plan, at the end of which, he disclaims all responsibility.

SIGMUND: That's ridiculous. I don't disclaim responsibility in three years.

LESTER: Well if you insist on continuous support, then Mrs Matchett should give you some of the furniture as collateral. We are talking *the* major pieces.

ALICE: That's crazy.

SIGMUND: I agree. That's crazy, Lester. The kids and her have to live, sleep, work, eat, sit in a chair, do whatever it is people do every day.

LESTER: *(To* SIGMUND*)* This is a battle. We're fighting here to divide the spoils.

SIGMUND: We sound like vultures.

ALICE: No room for sentiment here. You've come as far up here as you can go. This is a courthouse. She gets to keep all the jewelry Dr Matchett *gifted* her, without attachments.

LESTER: *(Writing it down)* No attachments.

ALICE: All liquid assets are divided equally since he is probably hiding what he *really* has in some bank in New Jersey.

LESTER: There is nothing in New Jersey.

SIGMUND: That's right.

LESTER: Try not to hold up progress, the two of you. We're committed to getting you a rock solid agreement. *(Quickly continuing)* He gets to keep the French Oriental.

SYBIL: Sigmund doesn't even *like* the French Oriental.

SIGMUND: I didn't even know we *had* a French Oriental.

SIGMUND	SYBIL:
What about WAM?	Women against Men?
Do you still belong to WAM?	Yes, they have a West Coast Branch;
	But Sig, it's nothing personal.

ALICE	LESTER:
All the real estate to her.	Then everything *in* the houses to him.

SIGMUND	SYBIL:
Oh nothing personal.	It's a political issue with me. And I joined because I was angry with you for making me punch a time clock.

ALICE	LESTER:
Who wants an empty house?	We are talking about value here, not utility.

(Above speeches should be timed to end at the same time. Though characters speak over each other, the lawyers don't miss a word.)

ALICE: He made you punch a time clock, Mrs Matchett?

SIGMUND: I just wanted to equalize the load. Why don't you ask her about the time she and her friends from WAM put a rabbit in the bed...a live one I might add.

SYBIL: Simply to remind you of *your* responsibility in the birth control process.

LESTER: She put a rabbit in your bed?

(The next section occurs rapidly.)

ALICE: And on the insurance, he adds the dismemberment amendment, God forbid.

LESTER: God forbid.

SIGMUND: God forbid!

ALICE: *(Writing)* So on this twenty-fifth day of August, the party of the first part agrees with the party of the second part...

LESTER: *(Breaking in)* You're really getting a fine agreement, Dr Matchett. Everything spelled out.

ALICE: So everyone goes away happy.

LESTER: Final check. *(Checking his list)* Routine clauses on cohabitation and other deviations from the norm will in effect negate this contract.

ALICE: Wipe it out.

LESTER: And we would simply start from scratch.

ALICE: *(Breaking right in)* Now if you'll both sign this paper, Mr Ostermeyer and I will write it up and you could be divorced this afternoon. *(Pushing the paper at SIGMUND)*

LESTER: In the next hour.

SIGMUND: As simple as that. *(He does not sign right away but ignores the paper)*

ALICE: This agreement will not be considered final, of course, for six months, so both of you would have to wait that period to remarry.

SYBIL: To remarry...

ALICE: Most difficult settlement since Ford versus Ford. I can't believe it's almost over. Just sign here, Mrs Matchett... *(Holding out the paper to SYBIL)* ...and you'll be divorced, out in the world with the rest of us, out in the marketplace. You'll receive a xeroxed copy.

(SYBIL does not move to sign)

LESTER: *(To SIGMUND)* Just sign your John Doe here and you're a free man.

SIGMUND: *(Interior)* The night she left I kept thinking, if I get up the next morning and start the day with orange juice, everything will be okay.

SYBIL: *(Interior)* I didn't stop crying until Indiana. And the moonlight does not shine along the Wabash. The kids were silent all the way across the country. Not one fight. Thank you, I thought, for something. By the time we got to the Black Hills, I couldn't remember why we had started out.

SIGMUND: Sybil, we're all alone in our lives and nobody knows. We could die of something and no one would know.

SYBIL: I know.

LESTER: People are waiting to lock up. *(Holding out the document to SIGMUND)* X marks the spot. *(Handing him the pen)*

(Pause. SIGMUND signs.)

ALICE: Mrs Matchett... *(Holding out the document and pen)* Your signature... *(Pause)* AND IT'S....

(SYBIL signs.)

ALICE: OVER!

LESTER: It's over, Dr Matchett! It's over!

SYBIL: *(Quietly)* It's over.

SIGMUND: All over.

SYBIL: Wait a minute! You forgot the children!

LESTER: The children.

ALICE: The children.

SIGMUND: How could you forget the children?

ALICE: Well they're *your* children.

LESTER: You could have reminded us.

ALICE: *(Holding out her lists)* Look at all these items we're juggling. You need the memory of an elephant. *(Looking over the list)*. She got the swings on the outdoor equipment clause.

LESTER: So he gets the children, no strings attached.

SYBIL: Wait a minute. I'm not giving up any children.

LESTER: We all have to make do with partial rewards.

SYBIL: Tell it to Santa Claus.

SIGMUND: The children are hers.

ALICE: I move we put the children on a rider.

LESTER: *(Writing) Ride* the children.

SIGMUND: I mean they're ours, but I can't make the home Sybil does. I think we'll arrange this between us. Don't you think, Sybil?

SYBIL: We prefer to arrange matters between us privately. *(Pause)* We'll separate and divide them ourselves.

LESTER: *(Packing up)* Everything then is in order and accord.

ALICE: *(Packing up)* Congratulations, Mr Ostermeyer. *(Shaking his hand)*

LESTER: *(Saluting)* I salute you, Mrs Bailey. A lovely agreement.

ALICE: Good afternoon, Dr Matchett, Mrs... *(Correcting herself)* Sybil Matchett. *(Looking out the window)* Blue skies, white clouds, birds singing... It's a beautiful day for a divorce.

LESTER: An exquisite day for a divorce.

(LESTER and ALICE exit.)

(Pause)

SIGMUND: And it's over.

SYBIL: All over

SYBIL: *(Interior)* It was green and white outside and in. Afterwards, we made love, of course.

SIGMUND: *(Interior)* I'll love you forever, I said. The name of the boat was "Someday".

SYBIL: Sometimes when I'm on a date I call the man Sigmund by mistake. I forget maybe I'll always forget, or never forget... Oh God, I'm embarrassed. Could you give me a lift to the airport?

SIGMUND: Maybe you never will. When I go to bed at night I always make sure the pillows are together, even though no one's there. Come on, Sybil. *(Pause)* To the airport.

SYBIL: To the airport.

                                    END OF PLAY

www.ingramcontent.com/pod-product-compliance
Lightning Source LLC
Chambersburg PA
CBHW070807100426
42742CB00012B/2281